John Edgar McFadyen

The Wisdom Books (Job, Proverbs, Ecclesiastes)

Also Lamentations and the Song of Songs in modern Speech and Rhythmical Form

John Edgar McFadyen

The Wisdom Books (Job, Proverbs, Ecclesiastes)
Also Lamentations and the Song of Songs in modern Speech and Rhythmical Form

ISBN/EAN: 9783337040840

Printed in Europe, USA, Canada, Australia, Japan

Cover: Foto ©ninafisch / Pixelio.de

More available books at **www.hansebooks.com**

THE WISDOM BOOKS
(JOB, PROVERBS, ECCLESIASTES)

ALSO

LAMENTATIONS

AND

THE SONG OF SONGS

IN MODERN SPEECH
AND RHYTHMICAL FORM

BY

JOHN EDGAR McFADYEN, D.D.

PROFESSOR OF OLD TESTAMENT LANGUAGE, LITERATURE, AND THEOLOGY
UNITED FREE CHURCH COLLEGE, GLASGOW

AUTHOR OF "THE PROBLEM OF PAIN" (A STUDY IN THE BOOK OF JOB),
"THE PSALMS IN MODERN SPEECH," "A CRY FOR JUSTICE" (A STUDY
IN THE BOOK OF AMOS), "THE PRAYERS OF THE BIBLE," "THE CITY
WITH FOUNDATIONS," ETC.

LONDON
JAMES CLARKE & CO., 13 & 14, FLEET STREET, E.C.

TO THE

REV. JOHN NEIL, D.D.

MINISTER OF WESTMINSTER CHURCH, TORONTO ;
MODERATOR OF THE FORTY-THIRD GENERAL
ASSEMBLY OF THE PRESBYTERIAN CHURCH IN
CANADA (1917-18)

MY FRIEND AND FORMER PASTOR
THIS VOLUME IS DEDICATED
WITH VERY CORDIAL REGARD

PREFACE

THE generous reception accorded to *The Psalms in Modern Speech and Rhythmical Form* leads me to hope that the translation of other parts of the Old Testament, executed along similar lines, may be not unwelcome. This volume and its predecessor together comprise all the specifically poetical books of the Old Testament—that is, all the poetry that lies outside the prophetic literature and the sporadic poems or fragments of poems embedded in the historical books. In this volume, as in the other, I have endeavoured to let the writers speak to us in the language of to-day, and also with something of the music which haunts their words in their original form. Perhaps no translation of a poem can ever do it adequate justice ; but even approximate justice is impossible where cadence and rhythm and all that make it a poem are deliberately ignored. For while thought is as essential to poetry as to prose, these things are of its essence too.

Two impressions rise upon the mind from this conspectus of Hebrew poetry. One is that of its astonishing range and variety. Here, if anywhere, we come upon the humanism of the Bible ; and here, if anywhere, Hebrew literature challenges comparison with the literatures of other peoples. These books breathe the spirit of the great world. The pessimism of Ecclesiastes is the voice of the weary souls of a hundred lands. The Book of Job, with its intense dramatic quality and its

Preface

fierce and resolute wrestlings with the problems that still baffle the minds of men ; the love-poetry of the Song of Songs, fragrant with the breath of spring, touched with a passionate appreciation of nature in her every mood, athrill from end to end with the love of man for maid and maid for man : these and other things in this collection are not of yesterday only, but for to-day and for ever.

The other impression is that of the distance that separates the Old Testament from the New. The challenges of Job, the utilitarianism of Proverbs, the scepticism of Ecclesiastes, the romanticism of the Song, the melancholy of Lamentations, are all equally inconceivable on the pages of the New Testament ; and they help us to feel very vividly the difference that Jesus made.

The notes in this volume are more numerous than in the other, because the text of these books is very frequently difficult to the point of desperation, and it is no part of an interpreter's business to create the impression of certainty, where the evidence is inadequate, ambiguous or baffling. But I have reduced the notes to the barest minimum, giving only such as justify the translation, explain allusions, or briefly elucidate obscurities : they are in no sense a substitute for exegesis. Commentaries will always be necessary, but too often they shadow the text instead of illuminating it. The ideal commentary would be a perfect translation : for then, without intervening explanation, the ancient writer would make his own immediate impression, and speak home to the hearts of his readers as a man speaks to his friend.

JOHN E. MCFADYEN.

CONTENTS

JOB

THE PROLOGUE

	PAGE
Job's Piety and Prosperity (i. 1-5)	17
The Heavenly Council. Satan is permitted to test the Quality of Job's Piety (i. 6-12)	17
The Blows Fall (i. 13-22)	18
The Second Council (ii. 1-7a)	19
The Second Test (ii. 7b-10)	20
Job's Friends Come to Comfort Him (ii. 11-13)	21

ACT I

Job's Lament and Longing for Death (iii.)	22
Eliphaz's Comfortable Exhortation and Revelation (iv. and v.)	23
Job's Denunciation of Hollow Friendship. His Challenge of God and his Longing to be Gone (vi. and vii.)	27
Bildad's Appeal to the Teaching of Tradition (viii.)	30
Job's Challenge of Immoral Omnipotence (ix. and x.)	32
Zophar's Appeal to the Unsearchable Wisdom of God (xi.)	36
Job's Independent Criticism of this World and his Glimpse Beyond It (xii.-xiv.)	37

ACT II

Eliphaz's Appeal to the Unadulterated Doctrine of the Past (xv.)	43
Job's Cry to the Witness in Heaven (xvi. and xvii.)	45
Bildad's Picture of the Sure and Terrible Doom of the Wicked (xviii.)	48

Contents

	PAGE
JOB'S SUBLIME FAITH IN HIS FUTURE VINDICATION (xix.)	49
ZOPHAR'S WARNING AND INNUENDO THAT HEAVEN AND EARTH HAVE ALREADY WITNESSED AGAINST JOB (xx.)	51
JOB'S FIERCE INDICTMENT OF THE EXISTING ORDER (xxi.)	53

ACT III

ELIPHAZ'S CRUEL AND BASELESS CHARGES (xxii.)	56
JOB'S SECOND SUSTAINED INDICTMENT OF THE EXISTING ORDER (xxiii. and xxiv.)	58
BILDAD'S DECLARATION OF GOD'S WISDOM AND POWER (xxv. and xxvi.)	61
THE LAST CLASH—BETWEEN JOB AND ZOPHAR (xxvii.)	62
JOB'S GREAT DEFENCE AND HIS LAST APPEAL (xxix.-xxxi.)	64

ACT IV

THE ANSWER OF THE ALMIGHTY (xxxviii., xxxix., xl. 2, 8-14)	71
JOB'S HUMBLE AND PENITENT REPLY (xl. 3-5, xlii. 2-6)	76

THE EPILOGUE

THE FRIENDS REBUKED (xlii. 7-9)	78
THE RESTORATION OF JOB (xlii. 10-17)	78

ELIHU'S INTERPRETATION OF SUFFERING (xxxii.-xxxvii.)	80
THE MYSTERY OF THE DIVINE WISDOM (xxviii.)	92
THE HIPPOPOTAMUS (xl. 15-24)	94
THE CROCODILE (xli.)	94

PROVERBS

ON THE WORTH OF WISDOM (i.-ix.)

THE AIM OF THE BOOK (i. 1-6)	99
THE MOTTO OF THE BOOK (i. 7)	99

Contents

	PAGE
EXHORTATION AND WARNING (i. 8-19)	99
THE APPEAL OF WISDOM (i. 20-33)	100
THE BLESSED FRUITS OF WISDOM (ii.)	101
THE WISDOM OF TRUSTING AND HONOURING THE LORD (iii. 1-10)	103
THE WORTH OF WISDOM (iii. 11-20)	103
THE SECURITY THAT COMES FROM WISDOM (iii. 21-35)	104
THE EXCELLENCE AND BENEFICENT POWER OF WISDOM (iv.)	105
THE WRONG AND FOLLY OF IMPURITY (v.-vii.)	107
THE DEADLY POWER OF AN EVIL WOMAN (v. 1-14)	107
EXHORTATION TO FIDELITY (v. 15-23)	108
WARNING AGAINST THE ADULTERESS (vi. 20-35)	108
ANOTHER WARNING (vii.)	110
THE INVITATION AND THE REWARDS OF WISDOM (viii.)	111
WISDOM'S APPEAL TO MEN (viii. 1-21)	111
WISDOM'S ANCIENT ORIGIN (viii. 22-31)	113
WISDOM'S CONCLUDING APPEAL (viii. 32-36)	113
THE TWO HOSTESSES—WISDOM AND FOLLY (ix.)	114
THE INVITATION OF WISDOM (ix. 1-6)	114
THE INVITATION OF FOLLY (ix. 13-18)	114
A GROUP OF APHORISMS (ix. 7-12)	115
WARNINGS	115
AGAINST SURETYSHIP (vi. 1-5)	115
AGAINST INDOLENCE (vi. 6-11)	116
AGAINST UNDERHAND MISCHIEF-MAKING (vi. 12—15)	116
SEVEN DETESTABLE THINGS (vi. 16-19)	116
FIRST COLLECTION OF PROVERBS (x. 1-xxii. 16)	118
SECOND COLLECTION OF PROVERBS (xxii. 17-xxiv. 22)	143
APPENDIX TO THE SECOND COLLECTION OF PROVERBS (xxiv. 23-34)	148

Contents

	PAGE
THIRD COLLECTION OF PROVERBS (xxv.-xxix.)	150

COLLECTION OF BRIEF DISCOURSES AND APHOR-
ISMS (xxx. and xxxi.) 160
THE WEARY WORLD-PROBLEM (xxx. 1-6) . . 160
A PRAYER FOR PRESERVATION ALIKE FROM
WEALTH AND POVERTY (xxx. 7-9) . . 160
AGAINST DEFAMATION (xxx. 10) . . . 161
FOUR EVIL TYPES (xxx. 11-14) . . . 161
FOUR INSATIABLE THINGS (xxx. 15, 16) . . 161
AGAINST CONTEMPT OF PARENTS (xxx. 17) . 161
FOUR MYSTERIOUS THINGS (xxx. 18, 19) . . 162
FOUR INTOLERABLE THINGS (xxx. 21-23) . . 162
FOUR THINGS LITTLE BUT WISE (xxx. 24-28) . 162
FOUR STATELY THINGS (xxx. 29-33) . . 162
AGAINST IMMORALITY AND INTEMPERANCE (xxxi.
1-9) 163
THE IDEAL HOUSEWIFE (xxxi. 10-31) . . 163

ECCLESIASTES

THE FUTILITY AND MONOTONY OF NATURE AND
OF HUMAN LIFE (i. 1-8) . . . 169
THE FUTILITY OF THE SEARCH AFTER KNOW-
LEDGE (i. 9-18) 169
THE FUTILITY OF THE SEARCH AFTER PLEASURE
(ii. 1-12) 170
THE FUTILITY OF WISDOM (ii. 13-17) . . 171
THE FUTILITY OF WORK (ii. 18-26) . . . 172
THE FUTILITY OF HUMAN EFFORT IN THE LIGHT
OF THE FIXED ORDER OF THE WORLD
(iii. 1-15) 173
THE FUTILITY OF HOPING FOR THE REDRESS OF
INJUSTICE IN SOME FUTURE WORLD
(iii. 16-22) 174
MAN'S INHUMANITY TO MAN (iv. 1-3) . . 175
THE TAINT OF JEALOUSY (iv. 4) . . . 176
THE WISDOM OF UNAMBITIOUS QUIET (iv. 5, 6) . 176
THE FUTILITY AND MISERY OF LONELINESS
(iv. 7-12) 176

Contents

	PAGE
THE FUTILITY OF WISDOM—AN ILLUSTRATION (iv. 13-16)	177
WARNINGS AGAINST INSINCERITY AND RASHNESS IN THE DISCHARGE OF RELIGIOUS DUTIES (v. 1-7)	177
THE PREVALENCE OF OPPRESSION (v. 8, 9)	178
THE FUTILITY OF WEALTH (v. 10-20)	178
THE FUTILITY OF WEALTH WITHOUT THE POWER TO ENJOY (vi. 1-9)	179
THE FUTILITY OF THE STRUGGLE WITH DESTINY (vi. 10-12)	180
COUNSELS FOR CONDUCT (vii. 1-14)	180
THE FOLLY OF EXTREMES (vii. 15-22)	181
WOMAN A DELUSION AND A SNARE (vii. 23-29)	182
REFLECTIONS UPON DESPOTISM (viii. 1-9)	183
THE FUTILITY OF LOOKING FOR A MORAL ORDER IN THIS WORLD, AND THERE IS NO OTHER (viii. 10-ix. 6)	184
THE WISDOM OF ENJOYMENT (ix. 7-10)	185
THE ELEMENT OF CHANCE IN LIFE (ix. 11, 12)	186
THE PLACE OF WISDOM IN POPULAR ESTEEM (ix. 13-18)	186
A TOPSY-TURVY WORLD (x. 5-7)	187
A COLLECTION OF PROVERBS (x. 1-4, 8-xi. 6)	187
REJOICE, YOUNG MAN, IN THY YOUTH: FOR THE SORROWS OF AGE ARE MANY AND SURE (xi. 7-xii. 8)	189
A LATER ADDITION IN PRAISE OF THE BOOK, AND, IN GENERAL, OF WISDOM (xii. 9-14)	191

LAMENTATIONS

JERUSALEM'S COMFORTLESS DOOM (i.)	195
THE DIVINE JUDGMENT AND THE INCONSOLABLE SORROW (ii.)	199
LAMENT AND PRAYER (iii.)	204
LAMENT OVER THE FATE OF THE PEOPLE AND THEIR LEADERS (iv.)	208
JERUSALEM'S SORROWS AND PRAYER FOR DELIVERANCE (v.)	211

Contents

THE SONG OF SONGS

	PAGE
The Bride Praises the Bridegroom, Depreciates her own Beauty, and Asks where her Bridegroom is to be found (i. 1-8)	217
Bride and Bridegroom sing each other's Praises (i. 9-ii. 3)	218
The Happiness of the Bride (ii. 4-7)	219
A Spring Wooing (ii. 8-17)	219
The Bride's Dream (iii. 1-5)	221
The Bridegroom's Procession (iii. 6-11)	222
In Praise of the Charms of the Bride (iv. 1-v. 1)	222
In Praise of the Bridegroom (v. 2-vi. 3)	224
In Praise of the Bride (vi. 4-13)	227
In Praise of the Bride as she Dances the Sword-Dance (vii. 1-9)	228
The Bride's Longing (vii. 10-viii. 2)	229
The Incomparable Power of Love (viii. 5-7)	230
The Bride's Proud Reply to her Brothers (viii. 8-10)	231
The Two Vineyards (viii. 11, 12)	231
Conclusion (viii. 13, 14)	232
Notes on Job	235
Notes on Proverbs	249
Notes on Ecclesiastes	268
Notes on Lamentations	275
Notes on The Song of Songs	278
Bibliography	284

JOB

THE PROLOGUE (Chaps. I and II)

Job's Piety and Prosperity

i.
1   In the land of Uz[1] there was a man called Job—
    a man blameless and upright, who feared God and
2   shunned evil. He had a family of seven sons and
3   three daughters: and he owned seven thousand
    sheep, three thousand camels, five hundred yoke
    of oxen, five hundred she-asses, and a vast train of
    servants, so that he was the richest man in all the
4   East. Now his sons used to hold feasts day about,
    and they would send and invite their three sisters
5   to eat and drink with them; and when the cycle
    of feasts was over, Job used to send for them and
    prepare them for worship, rising early and offering
    burnt offerings for them all: for — said Job —
    Perchance my children have sinned
    And cursed[2] God in their heart.
    And this Job never failed to do.

The Heavenly Council. Satan is permitted to test the Quality of Job's Piety

6   Now on a certain day the heavenly Beings[3]
    came to present themselves before Jehovah, and
7   among them came Satan.[4] Then Jehovah asked
    Satan where he had come from, and Satan answered
    Jehovah thus, "From ranging the earth and from

8 walking up and down it." Then Jehovah said to Satan:
"Hast thou noted my servant Job,
    That on earth there is none like him—
A man blameless and upright,
    Who fears God and shuns evil?"
9 To this Satan made answer:
'But is it for nothing that Job fears God?
10 Hast Thou not Thyself fenced him and his house,
    And all he possesses on every side?
The work of his hands Thou hast blessed,
    And his substance abounds in the land.
11 But put forth Thy hand and touch all he possesses,
    And assuredly then to Thy face he will curse Thee."
12 Whereat Jehovah said to Satan:
"See! all he possesses is in thy power,
    But lay not thy hand on the man himself."
Then forth Satan went from the presence of Jehovah.

The Blows Fall

13 Now on a certain day, as his sons and daughters were eating and drinking wine in the house of their
14 eldest brother, suddenly a messenger appeared before Job with the tidings:
"The oxen were hard at the plough;
    And the asses were feeding beside them,
15 When Sabeans [5] fell upon them and seized them;
    The servants they slew with the sword —
    Only I alone am escaped to tell thee."
16 While *he* was still speaking, another came and said:
"The fire of God has fallen from heaven,

Job

And burnt to a cinder the sheep and the servants —
Only I alone am escaped to tell thee."
17 While *he* was still speaking, another came and said :
" Chaldeans,[6] formed into three bands,
Made a raid on the camels and seized them.
The servants they slew with the sword —
Only I alone am escaped to tell thee."
18 While *he* was still speaking, another came and said :
" Thy sons and thy daughters were eating and drinking
In the house of their eldest brother :
19 On a sudden a mighty wind
From the other side of the desert
Came and smote the four sides of the house,
That it fell on the young folk and killed them—
Only I alone am escaped to tell thee."

20 Then Job rose and rent his robe ; and, after shaving his head, he threw himself with these words prostrate upon the ground :
21 "Naked came I from my mother's womb,
And naked thither must I return.
Jehovah hath given, Jehovah hath taken :
The name of Jehovah be blessed."[7]
22 In all this Job committed no sin, nor did he charge God with unseemly dealing.

The Second Council

ii.
1 Now on a certain day the heavenly Beings came to present themselves before Jehovah, and among them came Satan to present himself before Jehovah.
2 Then Jehovah asked Satan where he had come from,

The Wisdom Books

and Satan answered Jehovah thus, "From ranging the earth and from walking up and down it."
3 Then Jehovah said to Satan:
"Hast thou noted my servant Job,
   That on earth there is none like him —
A man blameless and upright,
   Who fears God and shuns evil?
And still he clings to his honour —
   In vain hast thou set me on to destroy him."
4 To this Satan made answer:
"Skin for skin;
   All a man's goods will he give for his life.
5 But put forth Thy hand, touch his bone and his flesh,
   And assuredly then to Thy face he will curse Thee."
6 Whereat Jehovah said to Satan:
"See! he is in thy power,
   But take heed that thou spare his life."
7 Then forth Satan went from the presence of Jehovah.

The Second Test

And he smote Job from the sole of his foot to the
8 crown of his head with boils so grievous that he took a potsherd to scratch with; and, as he was
9 sitting among the ashes, his wife said to him:
"Art thou clinging still to thine honour?
   Curse God and die."
10 But Job said to her:
"Must thou too speak
   As foolish women speak?
We accept from God what is good:
   Shall we not accept what is evil?"
In all this Job was guilty of no sin of speech.

Job

Job's Friends Come to Comfort Him

11 When Job's three friends heard of all the misery that had come upon him, they travelled each man from his own place—Eliphaz the Temanite, Bildad the Shuhite, and Zophar the Naamathite ;[1] for they had made a tryst together to come to condole with
12 him and comfort him. But when they caught a glimpse of him at a distance they did not recognize him. Then every man of them wept aloud and tore his robe and scattered dust heavenwards upon
13 his head. Then they sat down beside him upon the ground seven days and nights, and no one said a word to him ; for they saw that his pain was very great.

iii.
1 Thereafter Job opened his mouth to curse his
2 day, and thus he began :

ACT I

Job's Lament and Longing for Death

iii.
- 3 Perish the day wherein I was born,
  And the night which announced that a man-child had come.
- 4a Utter darkness let that night be,
- 9b Looking for light, but finding none.
- 4b May God in the heights above ask not after it,
- 4c And may no beam shine forth upon it.
- 5 May darkness and gloom claim it for their own,
  And may the thick cloud rest upon it.
  Black vapours of the day affright it !
- 6 And let the thick darkness snatch it away.
  May it not be joined to the days of the year,
  Or enter into the tale of the months.
- 7 As for that night, let it be barren :
  May there never ring through it a cry of joy.
- 8 Accursed of sorcerers be that day —
  Of those that are skilful to stir up Leviathan.[1]
- 9a Dark be the stars of its morning twilight,
- 9c And never the eyelids of Dawn may it see ;
- 10 Since it shut not the doors of my mother's womb,
  And hid not trouble from mine eyes.

- 11 Why died I not at my birth,
  Breathe my last as I came from the womb,
- 16 Like a hidden untimely birth,
  Like infants that never see light ?

Job

12 Why on the knees² was I welcomed,
   And why were there breasts to suck?
13 For then had I lain down in quiet,
   Then had I slept and had rest —
14 With kings of the earth and with counsellors,
   Who built stately tombs³ for themselves,
15 Or with princes rich in gold,
   Who had filled their houses with silver.
17 There the wicked cease their tumult,
   There the weary are at rest —
18 Prisoners at ease together,
   Deaf to the taskmaster's voice.
19 There the small and the great are alike,
   And the servant is free from his master.
20 Why is light given to the wretched,
   And life to the bitter in soul,
23 To the man whose path is obscured,
   Who is hedged round about by God —
21 Such as long for death, but it comes not,
   And dig for it more than for treasure,
22 Who would joy o'er a mound of stones,⁴
   And rejoice, could they find a grave?
24 For my bread there comes to me sighing,
   My groans are poured out like water.
25 For the evil I fear overtakes me,
   The thing that I dread comes upon me.
26 Scarce have I ease or quiet
   Or rest, when tumult cometh.

Eliphaz's Comfortable Exhortation and Revelation

iv.
1   Then Eliphaz the Temanite answered and said:
2   May we lift up a word unto thee who art fainting,
     For who has the heart to restrain his speech?

The Wisdom Books

3   See! thou hast instructed many,
    And strengthened the drooping hands.
4   Thy words used to set up the stumbling,
    And strengthen the tottering knees.
5   But now that it comes upon thee, thou art faint;
    Now that it reaches thyself, thou art terrified.
6   Is not thy religion thy confidence,
    And thy blameless life thy hope?
7   Bethink thee: has an innocent man ever perished,
    Or when have the just been cut off?
8   It is those who plough wrong and sow trouble
    That reap it :—for this have I seen.
9   By the breath of God they perish,
    At the blast of His anger they vanish.
10 The lion roared, the hoarse lion thundered;
    But his young lion's teeth were broken.
11 So for lack of prey he perished,
    And the cubs of the lioness are scattered.

12 Now to me a word came stealing,
    And mine ear caught a whisper thereof,
13 In thoughts from the visions of night,
    When deep sleep falleth on men.
14 Fear came upon me and trembling,
    That made my bones all quake.
15 Then a breath passed over my face,
    The hair of my flesh bristled up.
16 There — it — stood.
        I could not tell what it looked like —
    This form before mine eyes.
        In the silence I heard a voice say:
17 "Can mortal be just before God,
    Or a man clean before his Creator?

Job

18 See! He putteth no trust in His servants,
   His angels He chargeth with folly.
19 How much more those whose houses are clay,
   Whose very foundation is dust,
   Who die before the moth,
20   Crushed between morning and evening,
   Bruised without any regarding it,
   Perished for evermore!
21 The cord of their tent is torn from them:
   They die—but without learning wisdom."

v.
1 Call now: will any one answer?
   To which of the saints[1] wilt thou turn?
2 For vexation killeth the fool,
   Indignation slayeth the simpleton.
3 I have seen a fool taking root,
   But his branch became suddenly rotten,[2]
4 His children were far from help,
   Crushed beyond hope of deliverance.
5 The hungry eat up their harvest,
   And the thirsty draw from their wells.[3]
6 For not from the dust riseth ruin,
   Nor out of the ground springeth trouble;
7 But man is born unto trouble,
   While the sons of flame soar above it.[4]
8 Were it I, I would seek unto God;
   My cause I would bring before God,
9 Who doeth great things and unsearchable,
   Marvellous things without number,
10 Who bringeth rain over the earth,
   And over the fields sendeth water—
11 Setting the lowly on high,
   And lifting the mourners to safety,

The Wisdom Books

12 Frustrating the plots of the crafty
   And robbing their hands of success,
13 So taking the wise in their guile,
   That their tortuous plans fail through rashness :
14 They feel in the day as in darkness,
   At noontide they grope as at night.
15 So the needy He saves from the sword,
   And the poor from the hands of the mighty.
16 Thus hope is born in the weak,
   And iniquity stoppeth her mouth.

17 Happy then the mortal whom God correcteth :
   So spurn not thou the Almighty's chastening.
18 For He bindeth the wounds He hath made,
   And His hands heal the hurt He hath dealt.
19 He will save thee in six distresses,
   In seven no evil shall touch thee.
20 In famine He frees thee from death,
   And in war from the power of the sword.
21 From the scourge of the tongue thou art safe ;
   Thou shalt fear not the onslaught of ruin.
22 At ruin and dearth shalt thou laugh,
   And the beasts of the field thou shalt fear not.
23 For the stones of the earth are thine allies,
   The beasts of the field are thy friends.
24 Thou shalt know that thy tent is secure,
   Thou shalt visit thy fold and miss nothing.
25 Thy seed thou shalt know to be many,
   Thine offspring as grass of the earth.
26 Thou shalt come to the grave in thy strength,
   As a sheaf cometh in in its season.
27 See ! this we have searched—so it is.
   We have heard it—lay thou it to heart.

Job

Job's Denunciation of Hollow Friendship. His Challenge of God and His Longing to be Gone

vi.
1   Then Job answered and said :
2   O could my vexation be carefully weighed,
       And my misery set in the balance against it !
3   For it is more heavy than sand of the sea,
       And therefore it is that my words are wild.
4   For the arrows of God Almighty are in me,
       My spirit drinketh their fiery poison.
       The terrors of God are arrayed against me,
7a   My soul refuseth to be at rest.[1]
5   Doth the wild ass bray as he nibbles the grass,
       And over their fodder do oxen low ?
6   Can a man eat that which is tasteless and saltless ?
       Is there any taste in the slime of the yolk ?[2]
8   O that I might have my request,
       That God would grant me the thing that I long for !
9   O that God would consent to crush me,
       To let His hand loose and cut me off !
10   So should I still have this for my comfort—
       Leaping for joy amid torture unsparing—
       That I had not concealed the words of the Holy One.
11   What is my strength, that I should endure ?
       Or what is mine end, that I should be patient ?
12   Is my strength the strength of stones ?
       Or was I created with flesh of brass ?
13   Behold ! I have no help in myself,
       And the power to achieve is driven from me.
14   To one who is fainting a friend should be kind,
       Even though he forsaketh the fear of Almighty

The Wisdom Books

15 But my brethren have dealt like a treacherous torrent,
   Like channels that overflow their banks,
16 Which are turbid because of the ice
   And the snow that hides within them ;
17 But, when they are scorched, they vanish :
   In the heat they are quenched from their place.
18 The caravans bend their course thither,
   Go up through the waste, and perish.
19 The caravans of Tema[3] looked out for them,[4]
   The companies of Sheba[5] kept hoping :
20 But their confidence brought them to shame ;
   When they came to the place, they blushed.
21 Such now have ye proved unto me :
   When ye look on the terror, ye shudder.

22 Did I ask you to give me a present,
   Or make me a gift of your substance,
23 To rescue me from the foe,
   Or from hand of the tyrant to free me ?

24 Teach me, and I will be silent ;
   Show me wherein I have erred.
25 How sweet are words that are true !
   But when *you* reprove, what is reproved ?
26 Is it *words* that ye mean to reprove ?
   But for winds[6] are the words of despair.
27 Would ye throw yourselves on the innocent,
   Or make an assault on your friend ?
28 Now look upon me, I pray you :
   I would surely not lie in your face.
29 O turn back[7]—let there be no injustice :
   Turn back, for the right is still mine.

Job

30 Is my tongue altogether perverted ?
　　Have I lost the sense of wrong ?

vii.
1　Hath man on the earth not a warfare,
　　With days like the days of a hireling ?
2　Like a slave that pants for the shadow,[1]
　　A hireling that longs for his wages,
3　So empty months are my portion,
　　And wearisome nights mine appointment.
4　I lie down, saying, " When cometh day ? "
　　When I rise, methinks, " When cometh even ? "
　　I am full of unrest till the dawn.
5　Worms and clods clothe my flesh ;
　　My skin grows hard and then breaks.

6　My days are more swift than a shuttle ;
　　They come to an end without hope.
7　O remember my life is but breath ;
　　Mine eye shall see good nevermore.
8　The eye that now sees me shall see me no more ;
　　Thine eyes shall look for me, but I shall be gone.
9　Like the cloud that is spent and that passeth away,
　　He that goes down to Sheol[2] shall come up no more.
10　He shall never come back to his house again,
　　And the place that was his shall know him no more.

11　So my mouth I will not restrain,
　　I will utter mine anguish of spirit,
　　Pour out mine embittered soul.
12　Am I a sea or a sea-monster,[3]
　　That upon me Thou settest a watch ?
13　When I look to my couch to comfort me,
　　To my bed for relief of my sorrow,

The Wisdom Books

14 Then Thou scarest me with dreams,
   And with visions dost so affright me,
15 That gladly would I be strangled :
   Death itself I spurn in my pain.
16 I would not live for ever :
   Let me go, for my days are but breath.

17 What is man, that so great Thou dost count him
   And settest Thine heart upon him—[4]
18 Visiting him every morning,
   And testing him moment by moment ?
19 O when wilt Thou turn Thine eyes from me,
   And leave me though but for a moment ?[5]
20 If I sin, how does that harm Thee,
   O Thou who art Watcher of men ?
   Why dost Thou make me Thy target ?
   Why burden Thyself[6] with me ?
21 Why not forgive my sin,
   And pass mine iniquity by ?
   For now I shall lie in the dust ;
   Thou shalt search, but I shall not be.

Bildad's Appeal to the Teaching of Tradition
viii.
1   And Bildad the Shuhite answered and said :
2   How long wilt thou utter these things—
    These thy blustering windy words ?
3   Is God a perverter of justice ?
    The Almighty subverter of right ?
4   If thy children, for sinning against Him,
    He has left to bear their transgression,
5   Yet seek thou thyself unto God,
    And supplicate the Almighty.

Job

6   And if thou art pure and upright,
      Thy righteous abode He will prosper ;
7   And, though thy beginning be slender,
      Thine end He shall greatly increase.

8   For inquire thou of past generations,
      Regard the research of the fathers :—
9   For *we* are but dullards of yesterday,
      Whose days on the earth are a shadow—
10 Shall *they* not give thee instruction,
      And bring forth words out of their heart ?

11 "Can[1] the rush shoot high without swamp,
      Or the reed grow up without water ?
12 While yet in its freshness, unplucked,
      Of all herbs it withers most quickly.
13 So end all who put God out of mind,
      And the hope of the hypocrite dies.
14 His confidence is but a thread,
      And his trust as the web of a spider.
15 He leans on his house, but it stands not :
      He grasps, but it cannot endure.

16 Like a plant[2] is he, fresh in the sunshine,
      With suckers that shoot o'er the garden.
17 Its roots are entwined round the well,
      It lays hold of its stone habitation,
18 But when it is ruined, the spot
      Denies having ever beheld it.
19 Thus its course ends in desolation
      And out of the dust springs another."

20 See ! God spurns not an innocent man,
      But He will not uphold evildoers.

21 He will yet fill thy mouth with laughter
   Thy lips with a shout of joy.
22 Thy foes shall be clothed with shame,
   And the tent of the wicked shall vanish.

Job's Challenge of Immoral Omnipotence

ix.
1 Then Job answered and said :
2 Yes, truly : I know it is so :
   But with God how can man urge his right ? [1]
3 Should *He* choose to contend against him,
   He could answer not one [2] in a thousand.
4 Wise-hearted and strong as He is,
   Who hath ever successfully braved Him ?
5 Mountains He moves without effort, [3]
   He turns them about in His anger.
6 He shaketh the earth from her place,
   And maketh her pillars shudder.
7 He speaks to the sun, and it shines not ;
   He setteth a seal on the stars.
8 He stretcheth the heavens all alone ;
   He treadeth the heights of the sea.
9 He maketh the Bear and Orion,
   The Pleiades and the southern chambers. [4]
10 He doeth great things and unsearchable,
   Marvellous things without number. [5]

11 Lo ! He passes me by all unseen ;
   Sweeps past—but I cannot perceive Him.
12 He seizeth, and who can prevent Him ?
   Who dare ask Him, " What doest Thou ? "
13 God will not withdraw His anger ;
   The helpers of Rahab [6] stooped under Him :

Job

14 How much less can I give Him answer,
    And choose out my words against Him?

15 Were I right, I could give Him no answer,
    But needs must entreat my Judge.
16 If I called, He would give me no answer;
    I cannot believe He would listen.
17 For He crushes me in a tempest
    With many a wanton wound.
18 He suffers me not to take breath,
    But with bitterness He fills me.
19 Is it question of strength? There He is.
    Or of justice? Then who will implead Him?
20 Am I right? Still mine own mouth condemns me.
    Innocent? He proveth me perverse.
21 Innocent I am—but I reck not.
    I spurn my life; 'tis all one.
22 And therefore it is that I say,
    " He destroyeth both guiltless and guilty."
23 When the scourge bringeth sudden death,
    The despair of the blameless He mocketh.
24 He hath given up the earth to the wicked;
    He veileth the face of its judges.
    If it be not He, who then?

25 My days are more swift than a runner,[7]
    They flee unillumined by joy.
26 They glide like the ships of reed,
    Like an eagle that darts on its prey.
27 If I vow to forget my plaint
    And to wear a bright face for a joyless,
28 I shudder at all my pains;
    I know Thou wilt not hold me guiltless.

29 I then am infallibly guilty,
     So why should I labour in vain ?
30 For though I wash me with snow,
     And cleanse my hands with lye,
31 Thou wouldst plunge me then in the mire,
     So that even my friends would abhor me.
32 Thou art not a man like myself,
     That we come into judgment together.
33 O for an umpire between us,
     To lay his hand on us both !
34 Let Him take but His rod from off me,
     And affright me no more with His terrors,
35 And then I would speak unafraid—
     For not such at heart am I.

X.

1 In my soul is a loathing of life,
    I will let my complaint loose against Him.[1]
2 I will say to God, " Do not condemn me,
    But show me the ground of Thy quarrel.
3 What dost Thou gain from oppressing
    And spurning the work of Thy hands ?
4 Hast Thou then eyes of flesh ?
    Or seest Thou as man seeth ?
5 Are Thy days like the days of mortals,
    Or Thy years like the days of man,
6 That Thou shouldest seek out my guilt,
    And make this search for my sin,
7 Though Thou knowest I am not guilty,
    And no treachery cleaves to my hand ?

8 Thy hands did fashion and mould me ;
    And now wilt Thou turn and destroy me ?

Job

9 Remember Thou madest me like clay,
    And back to the dust wilt Thou bring me?
10 Didst Thou not pour me out like milk,
    And curdle me after like cheese,
11 Clothe me with skin and with flesh,
    And knit me with bones and with sinews?
12 Life Thou didst grant me and favour,
    Thy Providence guarded my spirit;
13 While *this* was Thy secret heart,
    And this was Thy purpose, I know.

14 Do I sin? Then Thou dost observe me,
    And refuse to acquit me of guilt.
15 Am I wicked? Then woe is me.
    Just? I dare not lift up my head—
    Full of shame and drunken with sorrow.
16 If I rise, like a lion Thou huntest me,
    Working fresh marvels[2] upon me,
17   And bringing new witness against me.
    Thine anger with me Thou increasest,
    Thou musterest fresh hosts against me.

18 O why from the womb didst Thou bring me?
    O why died I not all unseen?
19 O to be as though I had not been,
    Borne from the womb to the grave!
20 Are the days of my life not few?
    O leave me to smile a little,
21 Ere I go to return no more,
    To the land of darkness and gloom,
22 To the land of murky darkness,
    Of gloom and utter confusion,
    Where the very light is as darkness."

The Wisdom Books

Zophar's Appeal to the Unsearchable Wisdom

xi.
1   Then Zophar of Naamah answered and said :
2   Should a voluble man go unanswered,
    A man who but babbles be justified ?
3   Must men hold their peace at thy bragging ?
    Thy mocking is no one to curb ?
4   Thou maintainest thy way to be pure,
    And thyself to be clean in His sight.
5   But oh that God would speak,
    And open His lips against thee,[1]
6   And show thee the secrets of wisdom—
    How marvellous[2] are her achievements !
    For then thou shouldst know that thy guilt
    God remembers not wholly against thee.[3]

7   Canst thou find out the deep things of God,
    Or come nigh the Almighty's perfection ?
8   It is higher than heaven—what canst thou ?
    Deeper than Sheol[4]—what knowest thou ?
9   Longer than earth is its measure,
    And broader it is than the sea.

10 When He sweeps past and puts men in durance
    And calls them to trial, who can turn Him ?
11 For well He knoweth vain men :
    He looks upon sin and He marks it.
12 Even a senseless man may be taught,
    As a wild ass's colt may be caught.[5]

13 Now, if thou wouldst prepare thy heart,
    And stretch out thy hands unto Him,
14 And put away sin from thy hand,
    And let wrong dwell no more in thy tent,

Job

15 Then thy face thou wouldst lift without blemish,
    And thou wouldst be steadfast and fearless.
16 Yea, thou wouldst forget thy sorrow—
    As floods that are passed wouldst thou think of it.
17 Brighter than noon would thy life rise,
    Thy darkness would be as the morning.
18 Secure wouldst thou be in thy hope :
    Thou couldst lie without trembling or care—
19 Lay thee down without one to affright thee,
    And many would sue for thy favour.
20 But the eyes of the wicked shall fail,
    The place of their refuge is perished.
    Their hope is—to breathe their last.

Job's Independent Criticism of this World and his Glimpse beyond it

xii.
1   Then Job answered and said :
2   Verily ye are the people,
    And wisdom shall die with *you*.
3   But, like you, I have understanding ;
    Who knoweth not things like these ?[1]
4   A[2] laughing-stock to his friend
    Is become one whose cry God had answered.
    A laughing-stock is the righteous ;
5   The blameless is doomed to disaster.
    The man of ease mocks at his fate :
    There are thrusts for the feet that are slipping.
6   It is tents of robbers that prosper,
    And those who vex God that are safe—
    Those who say, " Is not God in my hand ? "

7   But inquire of the beasts—they will teach thee ;
    The birds of the air—they will show thee :

The Wisdom Books

8 The creatures that crawl—they will teach thee;
   The fish of the sea—they will tell thee.
9 For which of them all doth not know
   That the hand of Jehovah[3] hath wrought this—
10 In whose hand are all living souls
   And the breath of all humankind?

11 Doth not the ear test words
   As the palate tastes food for itself?
12 Doth wisdom depend upon years,
   Understanding on length of days?
13 With Him is wisdom and might,
   Understanding and counsel are His.
14 See! He breaketh down, and who buildeth?
   Imprisons, and none can set free.
15 See! He holds back the floods and they dry;
   Then He hurls them on earth and confounds it.
16 With Him is strength and achievement;
   Deceived and deceiver are His.
17 The wise men of earth He makes foolish;
   The judges He turns into madmen.
18 The fetters kings rivet He loosens,
   And binds their own loins with a chain.
19 He leadeth priests barefoot away;
   Ancient families He overturneth.
20 He removeth the speech of the trusty;
   The elders He robs of discretion.
21 He poureth contempt upon princes;
   He looseth the belt of the strong.
22 He revealeth the deep things of darkness,
   The gloom-wrapped He bringeth to light.
23 He makes nations great and destroys them;
   Expands them, then hurls them to ruin.[4]

Job

24 Earth's chiefs He bereaves of their judgment;
  They wander in trackless wastes,
25 Where they grope in the unlit darkness,
  And stagger like drunken men.

xiii.
1 Lo! all this mine eye hath seen,
  Mine ear hath heard it and marked it.
2 What *ye* know, that *I* know too;
  I am not one whit behind you.
3 But I would address the Almighty—
  With God I am longing to reason:
4 For ye are smearers of lies,
  Good-for-nothing physicians—each man of you.
5 O that ye were but silent—
  Then might ye be counted as wise.

6 Now listen to this mine indictment,
  Attend to the plea of my lips.
7 Is it God that ye utter your lies for?
  Do ye speak your deceit for *Him*?
8 And to Him would ye show your favour?
  And God's is the cause ye would plead?
9 Were it well if He searched you out?
  Can ye mock Him as men are mocked?
10 For He will punish you sore,
  If ye secretly show Him your favour.
11 Shall His majesty not make you shudder?
  Shall the dread of Him not fall upon you?
12 Your maxims are proverbs of ashes;
  Your bulwarks are bulwarks of clay.

13 Be still, let me be: *I* will speak—
  Then upon me come what may.

14   I will take my flesh in my teeth;
         I will put my life in my hand.
15   See ! He slays me, I cannot endure ;
         But my ways will I defend to His face :
16   And this, also, shall be my salvation,
         That a hypocrite dare not approach Him.
17   Hear now my speech with attention,
         As I declare in your ears.
18   Attend as I set forth my case;
         I know that the right is with me.
19   And if any disputeth against me,
         Then I would be silent and die.
20   But two things alone do not unto me,
         Then I will not hide from Thy face.
21   Lift the weight of Thy hand from off me,
         And let not Thy terrors appal me :
22   Then call Thou, and I will answer ;
         Or let me speak, and answer Thou me.
23   How great is my guilt and transgression ?
         Acquaint me with my sin.
24   O why dost Thou hide Thy face,
         And count me as Thine enemy ?
25   Wilt Thou harass a leaf that is tossed ?
         Wilt Thou chase the withered stubble,
26   That Thou passest a judgment so bitter,
         Entailing upon me the sins of my youth ?
27   Thou dost fasten a block on my feet,[1]
         And set watch over all my ways.
         Round my roots Thou cuttest a line,[2]
xiv.
  5c Setting bounds that they may not pass ;
xiii.
28   While man[3] doth waste with decay,
         Like a garment devoured of the moth.

Job

xiv.
1 Man that is born of a woman
    Is of few days and filled with trouble.
2 He comes forth like a flower and he withers;
    He flees like a shadow and stays not.
3 On *such* dost Thou open Thine eyes?
    And *him* wouldst Thou bring to Thy judgment?
4 Who can bring from the unclean the clean?
    Not one is free from sin.[1]
5a Seeing, then, that his days are decreed,
5b   And the tale of his months is with Thee,
6 Look away, and let him have peace,
    To enjoy like a hireling his day.

7 For hope there may be for a tree:
    Though cut down, it may sprout once again,
    And the shoots therefrom need not fail.
8 Though its root in the earth wax old,
    And its stem be dead in the ground,
9 It may bud at the scent of water,
    And put forth boughs like a plant.
10 But the strong man dies and lies prostrate;
    Man breathes his last and where is he?
11 Like the floods of a vanished sea,
    Like a river dry and withered—
12b Till the heavens be no more, he awakes not,
12c   Nor ever is roused from his sleep.

13 O wouldst Thou but hide me in Sheol
    Out of sight, till Thine anger be past,
  And then call me to mind in Thine own set time!
14   If a dead man may live once again,
    I could wait all the days of my warfare
    Until my release should come.

The Wisdom Books

15 Thou shouldst call, and I would answer :
   Thou wouldst yearn for the work of Thy hands.

16 But now Thou countest my steps,
   And passest[2] not over my sin.
17 My transgression is sealed in a bag;
   Thou hast fastened secure mine iniquity.
18 But the very hills crumble to pieces,
   The rocks are moved out of their place;
19 Water wears stones to dust,
   The floods wash the soil away :
   So the hope of man Thou destroyest ;
12a   He lieth, to rise up no more.
20 Thou dost worst him for ever ; he passeth,
   Dismissed—with his face how changed !
21 Honour comes to his sons, but he knows not :
   Or shame, but he doth not perceive it.
22 But the flesh upon him feels pain,
   And the soul within him is sorrowful.

ACT II

Eliphaz's Appeal to the Unadulterated Doctrine of the Past

XV.
1 Then Eliphaz the Temanite answered and said:
2 Would a wise man pour forth windy answers
   Or fill with the east wind his breast?
3 Would he reason with profitless words
   And with speech that is all unavailing?
4 See! thou art destroying religion,
   Disturbing devout contemplation.
5 Thy guilt instructeth thy mouth,
   And thou choosest the tongue of the crafty.
6 Thine own mouth condemns thee—not I,
   And thine own lips are witness against thee.

7 Wast thou the first man to be born?
   Wast thou fashioned before the hills?
8 Wast thou one of the heavenly council?[1]
   Was wisdom revealed unto thee?
9 What knowest thou that we know not?
   What insight is thine and not ours?
10 With us are the grey and the aged,
   More mighty in years than thy father.

11 Dost thou spurn the divine consolations,
   The word that dealt with thee so gently?[2]
12 How fierce the emotions that sweep thee!
   And how thou flashest thine eyes,
13 As thou turnest thy breath against God
   Into words from thy rebel lips!

The Wisdom Books

14 What is man that he should be clean,
   Or just—one of woman born?
15 See! He putteth no trust in His saints,[3]
   And the heavens are not clean in His sight:
16 How much less one abhorrent and tainted—
   A man that drinks evil like water!

17 Now listen to what I will show thee,
   The thing I have seen I will tell—
18 Even tales that were told by the wise
   And not hidden from them by their fathers,
19 Who had the land all to themselves,
   When no stranger had yet come among them.
20 All his days is the wicked in pain,
   All the years for the tyrant appointed.
21 In his ears is the sound of terrors,
   In peace comes the spoiler upon him.
22 He cannot escape from the darkness
   And he is reserved for the sword,
23 Appointed as food for the vulture—[4]
   He knows that his doom is at hand.
   The day of darkness appals him;
24a Constraint and distress overpower him;
25 For he stretched out his hand against God,
   Played the warrior against the Almighty,
26 Running against Him stiff-necked
   With the thick of the boss of his bucklers,
24b Like a king prepared for the onset.
27 He covered his face with his fat,
   He set thick folds of flesh on his loins;
28 And he dwelt in desolate cities,
   In houses that none should inhabit.

Job

What *he* has won, others shall capture,[5]
29 His substance shall not endure.
   On the earth he shall cast no shadow.[6]
30*b* The[7] fierce heat shall wither his branches,
30*c* His fruit shall the wind whirl away.
31 Let him not trust his plant when it shoots,
   For the branch thereof shall be vanity.[8]
32 It shall wither before its time,
   Or ever its fronds become green.
33 His grapes he shall shed like the vine,
   And cast off like the olive his blossom.
34 For a barren tribe are the godless ;
   Tents of bribery the fire shall consume.
35 Big with mischief, they bring forth sin,
   And their belly matures with deceit.

Job's Cry to the Witness in Heaven

xvi.
1   Then Job answered and said :
2   Many things such as these have I heard :
   Ye are wearisome comforters—all of you.
3   Shall windy words[1] have an end ?
   What is it that provokes thee to answer ?
4   I, too, could speak like you,
   Were your soul in my soul's stead.
   I could weave words together about you,
   And shake my head at you.
5   I could strengthen you with my mouth,
   And encourage you with lip-comfort.
6   To speak is no check to my pain ;
   To keep silence—that easeth me nothing.
7   But now He hath wearied and dazed me ;
   My misery seizes upon me.

8 It rises for witness against me;
   My grief testifies to my face.
9 In His wrath He hath flung me down torn;
   He hath gnashed upon me with His teeth.
   My foes whet their eyes upon me;
10   With open mouth they gape.
   They insult me with blows on the cheek,
   Coming on in their masses against me.
11 To knaves God has given me up;
   Into wicked hands He has hurled me.
12 I was happy, when *He* took and shattered me;
   Grasped my neck, and then dashed me in pieces.
   He set me up for His target;
13   On all sides His archers beset me.
   He cleaves through my reins unrelenting;
   He pours out my gall on the ground.
14 One breach after another He makes on me,
   Rushing at me like a warrior.
15 Sackcloth I sewed on my skin,
   And my horn I have laid in the dust.[2]
16 My face is red with weeping,
   And over mine eye-lids is darkness—
17 Though wrong there is none in my hands,
   And though my prayer be pure.

18 O earth! cover not my blood;
   No rest let there be to my crying.
19 Behold, in heaven is my Witness,
   And I have a Sponsor on high.
20 My friends pour their scorn upon me,
   But my tear-stained eyes look unto God,
21 That He plead for a man with God,
   And for son of man with his Friend.[3]

Job

22 For when but a few years come,
   I shall go whence I shall not return.

xvii.
1 His anger hath ruined my days,
   And for me is left nought but the grave.
2 Delusion is surely my portion;
   On bitterness tarries mine eye.
3 Lay a pledge for me—Thou with Thyself:
   For who else would strike hands with me?
4 For their heart Thou hast hidden from wisdom,
   And therefore Thou wilt not exalt them.
5 One inviteth his friends to a feast,
   While the eyes of his children are failing.[1]

6 Thou hast made me the by-word of nations;
   They look upon me as a monster.
7 Mine eye is grown dim for vexation;
   My members are all as a shadow.[2]
11 My days pass away without hope;
   The desires of my heart are extinguished.
12 The night I turn into day,
   And the light is before me as darkness.
13 If I hope, then the grave[3] is my home,
   And my couch I have spread in the darkness.
14 I call to the pit, " My mother ";
   And unto the worm, " My sister."
15 Where then were that " hope " of mine?
   And my happiness who can espy?
16 Will it go with me down to the grave?[3]
   Shall we sink to the dust together?

The Wisdom Books

Bildad's Picture of the Sure and Terrible Doom of the Wicked

xviii.
1   Then answered Bildad the Shuhite and said :
2   When wilt thou end thy words ?
    Now consider, and *we* shall speak.
3   Why are we counted as beasts,
    And deemed by thee to be dullards ?

xvii.
8   Honest men thrill with horror at this :
    A pure man is roused by such godlessness.
9   But the righteous holds on his way,
    And the man of clean hands waxes stronger.
10a But turn thee hither and come,[4]

xviii.
4   Thou that tearest thyself in thine anger.
    For *thy* sake shall earth be made desert,
    Or rock be moved out of its place ?

5   Nay, the light of the wicked is quenched,
    And the flame of his fire shall not shine.
6   The light in his tent shall be dark,
    And the lamp o'er his head shall go out.
7   His great swinging strides become shortened;
    His own counsel maketh him stumble.
8   His foot is thrust into a net,
    So that over the net-work he sprawleth.
9   A snare shall take hold of his heel,
    And a trap shall close tightly upon him.
10 A noose lies concealed on the ground,
    And a trap on his path doth await him.
11 On all sides are terrors appalling,
    Pursuing him close at his heels.

Job

12 For him shall misfortune be hungry;
  Disaster is ready to throw him.
13 The pestilence gnaws at his skin,
  And the first-born of death[1] at his members.
14 Then, dragged from his tent in despair,[2]
  He is marched to the King of Terrors.
15 His house shall be haunted by ghosts;[3]
  On his homestead shall brimstone be scattered.
16 His roots shall be dried up beneath,
  And above shall his branches be withered.
17 From earth shall his memory perish;
  No name shall be his on the streets.
18 From the light he is thrust into darkness,
  And chased right out of the world.
19 Of his folk, neither kith nor kin—
  Where he sojourned, not one is left.
20 The west is appalled at his doom,
  And the east is stricken with horror.
21 Yea, such are the homes of the wicked,
  Of those who care nothing for God.

Job's Sublime Faith in his Future Vindication

xix.
1 Then Job answered and said:
2 How long will ye vex my soul
  And crush me to pieces with words?
3 These ten times ye have put me to shame,
  And set upon me unabashedly.
4 Well, be it that I have erred—
  Mine error abides with myself.
5 Or would ye be haughty to me,
  And insult me with your reproaches?

The Wisdom Books

6   Know, then, it is God that hath wronged me,
    And compassed me round with His net.
7   Behold ! I cry " Wrong "—but no answer ;
    I call—but justice is none.
8   My way He hath fenced round impassably,
    Darkness He sets on my path.
9   He hath stripped my glory from off me,
    And taken the crown from my head.
10 He hath torn me clean down—I am gone :
    He hath plucked up my hope like a tree.
11 He hath kindled His anger against me,
    And counted me one of His enemies.
12 On come His troops together ;
    They throw up a rampart against me.[1]

13 My brethren are gone far from me ;
    My friends have estranged themselves from me.
14 My neighbours have ceased to acknowledge me ;
    Guests of my house have forgotten me.
15 Maids of mine count me a stranger ;
    An alien am I in their sight.
16 To my servant I call, but he answers not,
    Till with my mouth I entreat him.
17 My breath is strange to my wife,
    And my stench[2] to mine own very children.[3]
18 Yea, even young boys despise me,
    And mock when I try to rise.
19 All mine intimate friends abhor me ;
    The man whom I love turns against me.
20 My skin clings to my bones ;
    I escape with my flesh[4] in my teeth.

21 Have pity, have pity, my friends ;
    For the hand of God hath touched me.

Job

22 Why do *ye* persecute me like—God,
   And devour my flesh insatiably?

23 O that my words were now written,
   That they were inscribed in a book,
24 That with iron pen and with lead
   On a rock they were graven for ever.

25 I know that there liveth a Champion,[5]
   Who will one day stand over my dust;
26 Yea, Another shall rise as my Witness,[6]
   And, as Sponsor, shall I behold—God;
27 Whom mine eyes shall behold,[7] and no stranger's.
   My heart[8] is faint in my bosom.
28 But if ye are determined to hunt me,
   And in *me* find the root of the matter,
29 Then dread ye the sword for yourselves;
   For wrath[9] shall destroy the ungodly.[10]

Zophar's Warning and Innuendo that Heaven and Earth have already Witnessed against Job

XX.
1 Then Zophar the Naamathite answered and said:
2 Nay, not so do my thoughts make answer;
   And therefore my heart is uproused.
3 Must I hear thine insulting reproof,
   While mere breath without sense is thine answer?

4 Knowest thou not this from of old,
   From the time there were men on the earth,
5 That the song of the wicked is short,
   And the hypocrite's joy but a moment?
6 Though his majesty mount to the heavens,
   And his head reach unto the clouds,

The Wisdom Books

7 He shall utterly perish like dung ;[1]
  Those that knew him shall ask, " Where is he ? "
8 Like a dream he shall fly beyond finding,
  Dispelled like a vision of night.
9 No more shall the eye see that saw him ;
  His place shall behold him no more.
10 His sons shall be crushed by privation ;
  His wealth shall his children restore.[2]
11 The vigour of youth filled his bones,
  But with him it shall lie in the dust.

12 Though evil be sweet in his mouth,
  As he keeps it hid under his tongue ;
13 Though he spare it and let it not go,
  But still holdeth it back in his mouth ;
14 Yet his food in his stomach is turned ;
  It is poison of asps within him.
15 The wealth that he swallowed he vomits ;
  God casteth it forth from his belly.
16 The poison of asps he has sucked,
  And the tongue of the viper shall slay him.
17 No rivers of oil shall he see,
  No torrents of honey and butter.
18 His increasing gain brings him no gladness ;
  His trafficking yields him no joy ;[3]
19 For he crushed down the gains of the poor,
  And he plundered the house that he built not.
20 His treasures have brought him no peace,
  And his precious things cannot deliver.
21 And since none has escaped his devouring,
  His own fortune shall not endure.
22 Brought to straits in the fulness of plenty,
  The fell force of trouble assails him.

Job

23 He[4] shall let loose His hot wrath against him,
    And terrors shall rain down upon him.
24 As he flees from the weapon of iron,
    The bronze bow pierces him through.
25 The missile comes out at his back,
    And the glittering point from his gall.
    Terrors keep coming upon him;
26   Deep darkness is stored up for him.
    A mysterious fire shall devour him,
    And ravage those left in his tent.
27 The heavens shall reveal his guilt,
    And the earth shall rise up against him.[5]
28 His house shall be swept by destruction,
    Accursed in the day of His wrath.

29 Such the wicked man's portion from God,
    God's heritage unto the rebel.

Job's Fierce Indictment of the Existing Order

xxi.
1   Then Job answered and said:
2   Hear now my word with attention:
    Your consolation[1] be this.
3   Suffer me, for I would speak also:
    Then, when I have spoken, mock on.
4   Is it man[2] that I would complain of?
    And why should I not be impatient?
5   Now listen to me; and, in horror,
    Lay ye your hand on your mouth.

6   When I think of it, I am confounded,
    And shuddering seizeth my flesh.
7   Why are wicked men suffered to live,
    To grow old and wax mighty in power?

The Wisdom Books

8 Their seed is established before them,
   Their offspring in sight of their eyes.
9 Their homes are strangers to terror;
   No rod of God is on *them*.
10 *Their* bull doth unfailingly gender,
   Their cow never loses her calf.
11 Like a flock they send forth their young children;
   Their boys and their girls dance.
12 They sing to the timbrel and lyre;
   At the sound of the pipe they make merry.
13 They finish their days in prosperity,
   And go down to Sheol in peace—
14 Though they said unto God, " O leave us,
   We desire not to know Thy ways.
15 Why should we serve the Almighty?
   And what is the good of prayer? "
16 See! their fortune is in their own hand:
   Nought He cares for the schemes of the wicked.

17 How oft is the lamp of the wicked put out?[3]
   How oft does disaster assail them,
   Or the pains of His anger lay hold of them?
18 How often are they as the straw before wind,
   Or like chaff that is stolen by the storm?

19 " God stores up his guilt for his children."[4]
   (" Nay," I reply) ; " let Him punish
   The man himself, that *he* feel it.
20 Let his own eyes behold his disaster,
   Let *him* drink the wrath of Almighty.
21 For what doth *he* care for his house,
   When his own tale of months is cut short? "
22 Will any teach knowledge to God,
   Seeing He judgeth (angels) on high?

Job

23 One dies with his strength unimpaired,
  In the heyday of ease and prosperity ;
24 Filled are his buckets with milk ;
  His bones at the marrow are moistened.
25 And one dies with soul embittered,
  With never a taste of good.
26 In the dust they lie down together ;
  The worm covers them both.

27 Behold ! I know your thoughts
  And your cruel devices against me,
28 In asking, " Where lives now the tyrant ?
  Where now doth the godless[5] dwell ?"
29 Have ye never asked those that travel ?
  Have ye never noted their proofs
30 That the wicked is kept from disaster,
  Is saved in the day of wrath ?
31 Who tells him his way to his face,
  Or requites him for what he hath done ?
32 And yet he is borne to the grave,
  And men keep watch over his tomb.
33 Sweet for him are the clods of the valley,
  And after him all men draw.[6]

34 Why then offer your idle comfort ?[7]
  Your answers leave nothing but falsehood

ACT III
Eliphaz's Cruel and Baseless Charges
xxii.
1 Then Eliphaz the Temanite answered and said
2 Can a man bring profit to God ?
   Nay, the wise man but profits himself.
3 Doth Almighty God care for thy righteousness ?
   Hath He gain from thy blameless ways ?
4 For thy piety would He chastise thee,
   Or enter with thee into judgment ?
5 Is not thy wickedness great ?
   Are not thine iniquities endless ?
6 Thou hast wrongly taken pledge of thy brother,
   And stripped from the naked their clothing.
7 No water thou gavest the weary,
   And bread thou hast held from the hungry.
8 The land was for him that was strong,
   And the man of rank made it his own.[1]
9 Thou hast sent widows empty away,
   Orphan arms thou hast broken in pieces :
10 And therefore are snares round about thee,
    And fear on a sudden confounds thee.
11 Thy light is vanished in darkness,
    And floods of waters are over thee.
12 Is not God in the heights of heaven ?
    And the tops of the high stars He seeth.
13 Yet thou sayest, " What doth God know ?
    Can He judge aright through the thick darkness ?

Job

14   The clouds hide Him, so that He sees not ;
      He walketh the vault of the heavens."
15   Wilt thou keep to the ancient way,
      Which men of sin have trodden,
16   Who untimely were snatched away.
      While the ground beneath ran like a stream?[2]
19   The righteous[3] rejoiced at the sight,
      And the innocent laughed them to scorn.
20   " Ah ! surely our foes are cut off,
      And the remnant devoured by the fire."

21   Now be friendly with Him and submissive,
      For this is the way to happiness.
22   Accept from His mouth instruction,
      And lay up His words in thy heart.
23   If thou humbly[4] turn to Almighty,
      And put away sin from thy tent,
24   And lay in the dust thy treasure,
      Ophir gold among stones of the brook,
25   That Almighty become thy treasure,
      And His instruction thy silver,
26   Then Almighty shall be thy delight,
      Thou shalt lift up thy face unto God.
27   He will hearken unto thy petition,
      And so shalt thou pay thy vows.
28   The thing thou decreest shall stand,
      And light shall shine on thy ways.
29   For He humbles the high and the proud ;
      But whose eyes are lowly He saveth.
30   The innocent man[5] He delivers,
      And saves for his cleanness of hands.

The Wisdom Books

Job's Second Sustained Indictment of the Existing Order

xxiii.
1 Then Job answered and said :
2 This day also[1] my plaint must be bitter ;
   His[2] hand on my groaning lies heavy.
3 O that I knew where to find Him,
   That I might come unto His throne,
4 And set forth my cause before Him,
   With arguments filling my mouth !
5 I would know with what words He would answer,
   And understand what He would say to me.
6 Would He use His great power in the contest ?[3]
   Nay, He would give heed unto me.
7 There the upright might argue with Him,
   And my right[4] I should rescue for ever.

8 Behold, I go east, but He is not :
   And west, but I cannot perceive Him.
9 I seek on the north,[5] but in vain :
   I turn south,[6] but I cannot behold Him.
10 But He knoweth the way that is mine ;
    I would come forth as gold, should He try me.
11 My foot hath held fast to His steps,
    And His way have I kept without swerving.
12 Not once have I strayed from His precepts ;
    His words have I hid in my bosom.[7]
13 But when *He* hath resolved—who can turn Him ?
    And what He desireth, He doeth.[8]

15 For this cause His presence confounds me,
    The thought of Him fills me with terror ;
16 For God hath weakened my heart,
    And Almighty confounded me clean.

Job

17 I am utterly lost in the darkness,
    And gloom enwrappeth my face.

xxiv.
1 Why doth God not fix seasons for judgment,[1]
    And His friends never see His (great) day ?[2]
2 The[3] wicked[4] remove the landmarks,
    They plunder the flock with the shepherd.[5]
3 They drive off the ass of the fatherless,
    Take the ox of the widow in pledge.
4 The poor they turn out of the way,
    And the needy must huddle together.
5 See! like the wild ass in the desert,[6]
    They roam forth in search of prey ;
    Their children eat bread of the jungle.
6 They reap the fields in the night-time ;
    They plunder the vines of the wealthy.
7 All night they lie bare, without clothing,
    With nothing to keep out the cold.
8 They are wet with the showers of the hills,
    And the rocks they embrace for a shelter.
9 The fatherless they tear from the breast,
    And the babe of the poor take in pledge.
10 They go about bare, without clothing,
    And, hungry, they pilfer the sheaves.
11 They press out the oil 'twixt the olive-rows ;
    The wine-vats they tread and then drain.
12 From cities and homes they are driven ;
    Their little ones[7] cry out for hunger,
    But God takes no heed of the wrong.
13 There[8] are those who rebel against light,
    Who recognise not His ways,
    But refuse to abide in His paths.

The Wisdom Books

14 In the evening the murderer rises
    To butcher the poor and the needy.
    The thief stalks abroad in the night.
15 With face muffled up in a veil,
    The adulterer watches for twilight,
    Assured that no eye can behold him.
16 In the darkness they break into houses;
    They shut themselves up in the day-time;
    For all of them hate the light.
17 Familiar[9] with gloomy ways,
    They seek for themselves the deep darkness,
18   And swiftly they glide on the waters.[10]

        His[11] portion of land shall be cursed,
19   Consumed by the drought and the heat,
        And flooded away by snow-water.
20 The streets of his place shall forget him,
    Shall think of his greatness no more:
    Like a dead tree shall he be uprooted.
21 For he did not good to the widow,
    No pity he showed to her babe;
22   And his power swept the helpless[12] away.
    Vengeance falls: he expects not to live,
23   He is hurled beyond hope of recovery;
    The tormentor is on his way.
24 His greatness is brief—he is gone;
    Like the mallow[13] he bends, he shrivels—
    Cut down like the top ears of corn.

25 And if not, who will prove me a liar,
        And reduce mine indictment to nothing?

Job

Bildad's Declaration of God's Wisdom and Power

xxv.
1 Then Bildad the Shuhite answered and said :
xxvi.
2 How well[1] thou hast aided the weak[2]
   And supported the arm of the strengthless !
3 How well thou hast counselled the foolish,[2]
   And shown thine abundance of wisdom !
4 Who inspired thee to utter such words,
   And whose spirit is it that comes forth from thee ?

xxv.
2 Dominion and fear are with *Him*.
   On His high places[1] He maketh peace.
3 His hosts—are they not beyond counting ?
   Whom doth not His ambush[2] surprise ?
4 How can man then be just before God ?
   How can one born of woman be pure ?
5 See ! the moon herself is not clear,
   And the stars are not pure in His sight :
6 How much less is man—a mere maggot ;
   And the son of man—but a worm !

xxvi.
5 Before Him in pain writhe the giants,[3]
   Whose home is beneath the waters.
6 Sheol is naked before Him,
   Uncovered lieth Abaddon.[4]
7 He stretcheth the North o'er the void,
   And He hangeth the earth over nothing.
8 In His thick clouds He tieth the waters,
   Yet the clouds are not torn with the weight.
9 He closeth the face of His throne,
   And over it spreadeth His cloud.

The Wisdom Books

10 A circle He drew on the deep,
    To the confines of light and of darkness.
11 The pillars of heaven fell a-rocking,
    Astonished at His rebuke.
12 By His power He stirred up the sea,
    By His wisdom He smote clean through Rahab.[5]
13 His breath made the heavens fair;
    His hand pierced the serpent that fleeth.[6]
14 See! these are the fringe of His ways;
    Yea, 'tis only a whisper we hear:
    Who can tell how mighty His thunder?

The Last Clash—Between Job and Zophar

Job

xxvii.
1 Then Job answered and said:[1]
2 As God Almighty liveth,
   Who hath wronged and embittered my soul—
3 For within me my life is yet whole,
   And the spirit of God in my nostrils—
4 I swear that my lips speak no falsehood,
   My tongue doth not utter deceit.
5 God forbid I should grant ye were right;
   I will cling to mine innocence till I die.
6 I maintain to the end I am guiltless;
   Not an hour of my life do I blush for.

   .   .   .   .   .

12 Ye have all with your own eyes seen it:
   Wherefore, then, this idle folly?[2]

Zophar

7 Perish[3] my foe like the wicked,
   Mine enemy as the unrighteous.

62

Job

8   For what is the hope of the godless,
       When God requireth his soul?
9   Will God give ear to his cry,
       In the day when distress comes upon him?
10 Will Almighty be then his delight?
       When he calleth, will God be entreated?⁴

11 I will teach you how God wields His arm,
       And not hide the Almighty's behaviour.
13 The wicked man's portion from God is this,
       And the lot the Almighty bestows on the tyrant:
14 If his children grow up, the sword claims them;
       His offspring are stinted for bread.
15 By death⁵ shall his remnant be buried,
       Their widows shall make no lament.
16 Though silver he heap up like dust,
       And prepare (costly) raiment like clay,⁶
17 Yet the just shall put on what he stored,
       And the silver shall fall to the innocent.
18 Like a spider's the house which he builded,
       Like booth which the vine-keeper maketh.
19 He lieth down rich, but he wakes not;
       He openeth his eyes, and he is not.
20 He is caught in a flood of terrors;
       In the night he is stolen by a tempest.
21 The east wind bears him away;
       It sweepeth him out of his place.
22 He⁷ hurleth at him without mercy;
       Fain would he escape from His hand.
23 His hands He clappeth at him,
       And He hisseth at him from His place.⁸

The Wisdom Books

Job's Great Defence and His Last Appeal

xxix. *The Happy Past*

1 Then Job answered and said :[1]
2 O to be as in months long gone,
    As in days when God used to keep me,
3 When His lamp shone over my head,
    And I walked by His light through the darkness ;
4 As I was in the days of mine autumn,
    When God protected my tent,
5 While still the Almighty was with me,
    And my children were round about me ;
6 When my steps were bathed in milk,[2]
    And the rock poured me rivers of oil !

7 When I went to the city gate,
    Or took up my place in the open,
8 The youths, when they saw me, hid,
    The old men rose and stood.
9 Princes refrained from speech,
    And laid their hand on their mouth.
10 The voice of the nobles was hushed,
    And their tongue would cleave to their palate.
21 They[3] hearkened to me and they waited,
    Kept silence till I should give counsel ;
22 After *I* spoke, they spake not again,
    My speech fell like rain-drops upon them.
23 They waited for me as for rain—
    Open-mouthed, as for latter rain.
24 When I smiled upon them, they were strengthened ;
    The light of my face cheered the sorrowing.
25 I chose out their way and sat chief,
    Enthroned like a king in his army.[4]

Job

11 I was blessed by the ear that heard me,
   The eye bore me witness that saw me;
12 For I rescued the poor when he cried,
   The fatherless and the helpless.
13 The wretched gave me their blessing,
   The widow's heart I made sing.
14 I put on the garment of righteousness,
   A robe and a turban of justice.
15 Eyes was I to the blind,
   Feet to the lame was I;
16 A father was I to the poor,
   And I searched out the cause of the stranger.
17 I shattered the jaws of the wicked,
   And hurled the prey from his teeth.

18 So I thought, " I shall die with my nest,[5]
   As the sand my days shall be many.
19 My root is spread out to the waters,
   All night lies the dew on my branches.
20 Within me my glory is fresh,
   And my bow is renewed in my hand."

The Awful Present

xxx.
9 But[1] now am I become their song,
   Yea, I am a by-word among them.
10 In horror they stand far aloof,
   And they spare not to spit at the sight of me.
11 He hath slackened my bow-string,[2] and humbled me,
   Flung down my banner before me.[3]
12 Against me His hosts stand up,
   They raise deadly ramparts against me.[4]
13 My path they tear up clean,
   My tracks they destroy altogether.

The Wisdom Books

His archers ring me around,
14   As through a wide breach they come in,
Rolling on in the midst of the ruin.[5]
15   Terrors are turned upon me ;
My weal is the sport of the winds,
And my welfare is passed like a cloud.
16   And now is my soul poured out,
The terrors of misery seize me.
17   The night boreth into my bones,
And the pains that gnaw never slumber.
18   From sore wasting my garment is shrunk ;[6]
It clingeth to me like my vest.
19   (God) hath plunged me into the mire,
So that I am like dust and ashes.
20   I cry, but Thou givest no answer ;
Thou standest and heedest me not.
21   Cruel to me art Thou turned ;
With the might of Thy hand Thou dost scourge me.[7]
22   Thou settest me to ride on the wind,
And I melt in the roar of the storm.[8]
23   For I know Thou wilt bring me to death,
To the house where all living assemble.

24   Yet sinking men stretch out their hand,
And cry for help as they perish.[8]
25   He whose days are hard—does he weep not ?
Is the soul of the needy not grieved ?
26   For instead of the good I had hoped for came evil,
Instead of the light I awaited came darkness.
27   My heart is hot and restless,
And misery daily confronts me.
28   I go with my sorrow uncomforted,[8]
Standing where jackals[9] are gathered.

Job

29 Brother am I to the wolves,
   And of ostriches the companion.
30 All blackened my skin peels from off me;
   My bones are burned with the heat.
31 So my lyre is turned into mourning,
   My pipe to the voice of lament.

The Defence and Final Appeal

xxxi.
1 A tryst I made with mine eyes
   To give no heed unto folly.[1]
2 For how doth the high God reward[2] it—
   The Almighty in heaven requite[2] it?
3 Is not for the wicked misfortune—
   Disaster for workers of wrong?
4 Doth *He* not see my ways,
   And number my steps every one?

5 If ever I walked with falsehood,
   Or my foot hath made haste unto fraud—
6 Let God only weigh with just balance,
   Mine innocence He must acknowledge—
7 If my step ever swerved from the way.
   Or my heart hath gone after mine eyes,
   Or spot hath cleaved to my hands,
8 Then what *I* sow may others enjoy,
   And all produce of mine be uprooted.

9 If my heart hath been lured by a woman,
   If I lurked at my neighbour's door,
10 May my own wife grind to another,
    And let others bow down upon *her*.
11 For that were an infamous crime,
    An iniquity calling for judgment,[3]

The Wisdom Books

12 A fire that devours to Abaddon[4]
  And would all mine increase consume.

13 Never spurned I the cause of my servant—
  Of man or of maid—when we strove.
15 Did[5] not He that made me make him,
  Did not One fashion us in the womb?

16 Ne'er denied I the wish of the poor,
  Nor brought grief to the eyes of the widow.
17 Never ate I my morsel alone,
  Without sharing thereof with the orphan.
14 Else what should I do, when God rose?
  When He visited, what should I answer?
18 For father-like, *He* brought me up[6] from my youth,
  And my Guide has He been from my mother's womb.

19 Never saw I one naked and perishing—
  Needy, with nothing to cover him—
20 But I warmed him with fleece from my lambs,
  And his loins gave me their blessing.

21 If, because I saw help in the gate,
  I have ever set hand on the innocent,[7]
22 Let my shoulder fall from its blade,
  And mine arm from the socket be broken.

24 Never set I my trust upon gold,
  Nor called the fine gold my confidence.
25 Mine abundant wealth never elated me,
  Nor all that my hands had gotten.

26 Never, watching the shining lights,[8]
  Or the moon as she walked in her splendour,

Job

27 Did my heart feel their subtle allurement,
    Or my hand throw a kiss to my mouth.

28 This, too,⁹ were a crime for the judges,
    For to God above I had lied :
23 The terrors of God would assail me,
    Before whose approach I were powerless.¹⁰

29 Ne'er rejoiced I at enemy's fall,
    Nor triumphed when evil befel him ;
30 Nor suffered my mouth to sin,
    By demanding his life in a curse.

31 The men of my tent will declare
    None has ever been stinted of food.
32 Not a stranger e'er lodged in the street,
    For I opened my doors to the wayfarer.

38 If¹¹ my land ever cried out against me,
    Her furrows all weeping together ;
39 If her strength I have drained¹² without cost,
    Or have poured out the life of her owner ;
40 Let thorns take the place of wheat,
    And foul-smelling weeds—of barley.

33 No fear of the crowd ever led me
    To hide my sin among men.¹³
34 No contempt of the clans ever scared me
    To stay behind closed doors in silence.

35 O for One who would listen to me.
    Behold ! there is my cross !¹⁴
    Let Almighty God give me His answer.
    O would that I had the indictment
    Mine Adversary hath written !

36 For, bearing it high on my shoulder,
    And winding it round like a crown,
37 Every step of my life I would tell Him,
    Like a prince I would enter His presence.

40c The words of Job are ended.

ACT IV

The Answer of the Almighty

The Wonders of the Inanimate World

xxxviii.
1 Then Jehovah answered Job out of the whirlwind and said:
2 Who is this, then, that darkeneth counsel
   By words that are empty of knowledge?
3 Gird up thy loins like a man:
   I would ask of thee—do thou enlighten Me.

4 Where wast thou, when I founded the earth?[1]
   Declare out of the depths of thine insight.
5 Dost thou know who appointed her measures,
   Or who stretched upon her the line?
6 Whereupon were her pedestals sunk,
   Or who laid her corner-stone,
7 When the morning-stars sang together,
   And the sons of God shouted in chorus?

8 Who shut in the sea with doors,
   When it burst its way out of the womb?—
9 When I gave it its robe of cloud,
   And its swaddling band of the dark cloud;
10 When I broke off its border for it,
   And set on it bars and doors,
11 Declaring, "Thus far, but no further,
   And here shall thy proud waves be stayed"?

The Wisdom Books

12 Didst thou ever give charge to the morning,
   Or appoint to the day-star her place,
13 To take hold of the skirts of the earth,
   And to shake out the wicked from off it?
14 It is changed as clay under the seal,
   And the world stands forth (bright) as a garment.[2]

16 Hast thou entered the springs of the ocean,
   Or walked in the depths of the sea?

17 Have the gate-ways of Death been unveiled to thee?
   Hast thou looked on the porters[3] of Hades?

18 The breadth of the earth hast thou noted?
   How great is it? Tell, if thou knowest.

19 Which way leads to the home of the light?
   And where is the place of the darkness?
20 Canst thou fetch it out unto its border,
   Or lead it back home to its house?
21 Thou wast born then, so doubtless thou knowest—
   The tale of thy years is so great!

22 Hast thou entered the store-house of snow?
   Hast thou looked on the guardians of hail,
23 Which I hoard for the time of distress,
   For the day of assault and of battle?

24 Which way are the vapours divided,
   That scatter on earth the cool water?[4]
25 Who cleft for the torrents a channel,
   A path for the flash of the lightning—
26 Sending rain on the desolate land,
   On the uninhabited desert,

Job

27 Thus gladdening the wilderness waste,
   And the thirsty land clothing with verdure?

28 Say, hath the rain a father?
   Or who hath begotten the dew-drops?
29 Out of whose womb issued the ice?
   And the hoar-frost of heaven—who hath borne it?
30 The waters are frozen like stone,
   And the face of the deep remains hidden.

31 Dost thou fasten the chain of the dog-star[5]
   Or loosen the bonds of Orion?
32 Dost thou bring out the stars[6] in their season?
   The Bear with her young dost thou lead?[7]
33 Dost thou lay down the law to the heavens,
   Or establish their rule in the earth?

34 Dost thou lift up thy voice to the clouds,
   That abundance of waters obey[8] thee?
35 Dost thou send on their mission the lightnings?
   To thee do they say, "Here we are"?
36 Who hath set in the fleecy clouds[9] wisdom,
   Or given to the meteor[9] insight?[10]
37 Who spreadeth the clouds out in wisdom?
   Who tilteth the pitchers of heaven,
38 When the dust runneth into a mass
   And the clods cleave firmly together?

The Wonders of the Animate World

39 Dost thou hunt for the lion[11] his prey
   Or the young lions' craving appease,
40 When low in their lairs they crouch,
   Lying in wait in the thicket?

The Wisdom Books

41 Who provideth at even[1a] his food,
    When his young ones cry unto God,
    Open-mouthed, for the meat that is lacking?

xxxix..
1 Dost thou fix the birth-times of the wild goats,
    Or watch o'er the calving of hinds?
2 Dost thou number the months they fulfil,
    Or determine the time of their bearing?
3 They cower and bring forth their young,
    Swiftly ridding themselves of their birth-pangs.
4 Their young ones grow strong in the open,
    Go forth and come back not again.

5 Who let out the wild ass free?
    Who loosened the bonds of the wild ass,
6 Whose home I have made the steppe,
    And the salt-land the place of his dwelling?
7 He laughs at the din of the city,
    No driver roars in his ears.
8 The mountains he scours as his pasture,
    And every green thing is his quest.

9 Will the wild ox be willing to serve thee,
    Or spend the night in thy crib?
10 Wilt thou fasten a rope on his neck?
    Will he harrow thy furrows[1] behind thee?
11 Wilt thou trust his magnificent strength,
    Or put him in charge of thy labours,
12 Expect him to come again
    And gather thy seed to thy threshing-floor?

13 The wing of the ostrich beats joyously,
    But her pinions and feathers are cruel.[2]

Job

14 For she trusteth her eggs to the ground,
   And she setteth them down in the dust,
15 Forgetting that foot may crush them,
   Or beast of the field tread upon them.
16 Her young she treats harshly, as strangers,
   Unmoved though her toil be in vain.
17 For God hath not dealt to her wisdom,
   Nor allotted to her understanding.
18 She scuddeth along in her flight,[3]
   At the horse and his rider she laugheth.

19 Dost thou give to the war-horse his strength,
   Clothe his neck with the quivering mane?[4]
20 Dost thou make him to leap like a locust,
   With snort that is splendid and terrible?
21 He paweth the valley exulting,
   As forth to the fight he fares.
22 He laughs undismayed at the terror,
   He turneth not back from the sword.
23 Against him the quiver may rattle,
   The glittering spear or the dart:
24 He devoureth the ground in wild rage,
   Without turning to right hand or left.[5]
25 At the trumpet alarm he saith " Ha ! "
   For he scenteth the battle afar,
   The thunder of captains, the shouting.

26 Doth the hawk soar aloft by thy wisdom,
   And spread out her wings to the south?
27 Doth the eagle mount up at thy bidding,
   And make her nest high on the mountains?[6]
28 The cliff is her home where she lodges—
   The peak of the cliff and the fortress,

29 She spieth her prey from the heights
    With those eyes that see from afar.
30 Her young ones suck up blood :
    Where the slain are, there is she.

The Rebuke

xl.
2 Shall[1] a caviller strive with Almighty ?
    He that argues with God—let him answer.
8 Wilt[2] thou disallow my right,
    And condemn me that thou mayest be justified ?
9 Hast thou an arm like God ?
    With a voice like His canst thou thunder ?
10 Now deck thee with pride and with majesty,
    Clothe thee with glory and splendour.
11 Pour forth the floods of thine anger,
    And all that is lofty abase.
12 Every proud one lay low whom thou seest,
    And crush thou the wicked beneath thee.
13 Hide them together in dust,
    And bind up their faces in darkness.
14 And *I* then will render thee praise
    That thy right hand hath won thee the victory.

Job's Humble and Penitent Reply

xl.
3   Then Job answered Jehovah and said :
4   Ah, how small am I ! What can I answer ?
    I lay my hand on my mouth.
5   Once indeed have I spoken ;—enough :
    Yea twice—but not ever again.

Job

xlii.
2 I acknowledge[1] that Thou hast prevailed;
   There is nothing too hard for Thee.
3b Therefore spake I without understanding,
3c   Of wonders beyond my knowledge.[2]
5 I had heard of Thee but by hearsay,
   But now mine eye hath seen Thee;
6 And therefore I spurn (my words)
   And repent in dust and in ashes.

THE EPILOGUE
The Friends Rebuked

xlii.
7 So after Jehovah had spoken these words to Job, He said to Eliphaz the Temanite, " My anger is hot against thee and thy two friends ; because, unlike my servant Job, ye have not spoken the
8 truth about me. But now, go to my servant Job with seven bullocks and seven rams, and offer them as a burnt-offering for yourselves, and my servant Job shall pray for you ; for, out of regard for him, I will not put you to confusion for your failure to speak the truth about me, as my servant Job has
9 done." So Eliphaz the Temanite, Bildad the Shuhite, and Zophar the Naamathite went and did as Jehovah told them, and Jehovah had regard unto Job.

The Restoration of Job

10 So when Job prayed for his friends, Jehovah changed his fortunes, giving him double of all he
11 had before. Then his brothers and sisters and old friends came—every one of them—and dined with him at his home ; and they condoled with him, and comforted him for all the misery that Jehovah had brought upon him. Besides, each of them made him a present of a piece of money and a gold ring.
12 Thus in the end Jehovah made Job more blessed

Job

than he was at the first—with his fourteen thousand sheep, six thousand camels, one thousand yoke of
13 oxen, and one thousand she-asses. Besides, he had seven sons, and three daughters whom he named
14 in the order of their birth Jemimah, Keziah, and
15 Keren-happuch. In all the world were no women found so fair as the daughters of Job, and their father made them sharers in his inheritance with their brothers.
16 After this Job lived a hundred and forty years. Thus he was spared to see not only his children, but his grandchildren—four generations.
17 Then Job died—old and full of days.

ELIHU'S INTERPRETATION OF SUFFERING
(xxxii.—xxxvii.)¹

xxxii.
1 Now these three men ceased answering Job, because he was righteous in his own eyes. Then
2 the anger of Elihu the son of Barachel the Buzite, of the family of Ram, was kindled; against Job was his anger kindled, because he had made himself
3 out to be more righteous than God. But his anger was kindled against his three friends as well, because they had condemned Job² without finding
4 any answer. Now, as they were older, Elihu had
5 waited while they were speaking with Job; but, on seeing that the three men had no answer to offer, Elihu's anger was kindled.

6 Then Elihu the son of Barachel the Buzite answered and said :
I am but young in years,
 While ye are aged men :
So I was timid, and feared
 To set my opinion³ before you.
7 I felt that days ought to speak,
 And that years gave the right to teach wisdom.
8 But the spirit enlighteneth⁴ men,
 The Almighty inspires them with insight.
9 It is not the old men that are wise,
 Nor the aged that understand truth ;

Job

10 And so, pray, listen to me—
   I, too, would set forth my opinion.

11a I awaited what you had to say,
11b   I lent mine ear to your reasons;
12a Yea, I gave heed unto you,
11c   While ye searched out what to say.
12b But see! none brought conviction to Job,
12c   Not a man of you answered his words.
13 Say not "Here we have come upon wisdom;
   'Tis God must confound him, not man."[5]
14 He hath not yet debated with me,
   Nor will I give him answers like yours.

15 Panic-stricken[6] they answer no more,
   Words have floated away from them.
16 Must I wait because they are silent,
   Stand still, and answer no more?
17 Nay, but I, too, will answer my share;
   I, too, will set forth my opinion.
18 For filled with words am I;
   The breath in my body distresses me.
19 Like wine without vent is my belly,
   Like new wine-skins ready to burst.
20 I must speak and so find me relief;
   I must open my lips and make answer.
21 I would show my favour to none,[7]
   And give flattering titles to no man.
22 Of flattery I know nothing—
   Else soon would my Maker remove me.

xxxiii.
1 But listen, Job, pray, to my words,
   And give ear unto all that I say.

2 Behold! I have opened my mouth;
   My tongue in my palate hath spoken.
3 My heart poureth forth words of knowledge;
   Unfeigned is the speech of my lips.
5 Then answer me this, if thou canst:
   Stand up and debate with me.
6 See! I am in God's sight as thou;
   I, too, was fashioned of clay.
4 The spirit of God hath created me;
   My life is the breath of Almighty.
7 See! no terrors of mine need appal thee,
   Nor shall *my* hand lie heavy upon thee.

8 Thou hast certainly said in my hearing,
   Thy voice I heard thus maintaining:
9 " Pure and sinless am I;
   I am clean, there is no guilt in me.
10 But *He* findeth pretexts against me,
   He counteth me as His foe.
11 He setteth my feet in the stocks,
   Keepeth watch over all my ways.
12 Behold! when I cry, comes no answer:
   God hideth Himself from men."[1]

God speaks to Men through Dreams and Visions
13 Now why dost thou plead against Him
   That He giveth thy words no answer?
14 For God hath one manner of speech,
   Yea two—and He doth not revoke it.
15 In a dream, in a vision of night,[2]
   " When deep sleep falleth on men,"[3]
   In slumbers upon the bed,
16 Then He opens the ears of men,
   And sendeth them fearful warnings,[4]

Job

17 To turn men aside from wrong,[5]
  And to bring human pride to an end—
18 To keep back man's soul from the pit
  And his life from descending to Sheol.[6]

God speaks to Men through Pain and Sickness
19 Or on bed of pain he is chastened,[7]
  And all his bones are benumbed.
20 His soul has a loathing of bread,
  And the daintiest food he abhorreth.
21 His flesh is lean and wasted ;
  His bones are all but bare.
22 His soul draweth nigh to the pit,
  And his life to the angels of death.

23 Then over him there is an angel
  Interpreter, one of a thousand,
  Who expounds unto man his chastisement,
24   Takes pity on him and says :[8]
 " Let him not go down to the pit :
  I have found (for his soul) a ransom."
25 Then his flesh becomes fresher than child's,
  He returns to the days of his youth.
26 He prays unto God with acceptance,
  He looks on His face with joy,
  Tells the story of his salvation,
27   And sings before men this song :
 " I have sinned and perverted the right,
  Yet He hath not requited my sin.
28 He hath ransomed my soul from the pit,
  That alive I behold the light."

29 See ! all these things God doeth,
  Twice, yea thrice, with a man,

The Wisdom Books

30 To bring back his soul from the pit,
   With the light of life's sunshine upon him.
31 Be attentive, Job, listen to me ;
   Be thou silent, and I will speak.
32 If aught thou canst say, then answer me :
   Speak, for my wish is to clear thee.
33 But if not, listen thou unto me :
   Be silent, while I teach thee wisdom.

xxxiv.
1 Then Elihu went on :
2 Listen, ye wise, to my words,
   And give ear to me, ye that have knowledge.
3 For the ear is the tester of words
   As the palate the taster[1] of food.
4 Let us choose for ourselves what is right,
   Recognise by ourselves what is good.
5 For Job claimeth to be in the right :
   " God," he says, " hath deprived me of justice.
6 Though right, I am counted a liar ;
   And though sinless, He wounds me past healing."
7 Where is the man like Job
   That drinketh up scorning like water,
8 That leagues with the workers of wrong,
   And that walketh with wicked men ?
9 For he saith that a man hath no profit
   From being the friend of God.

God watches over the Moral Order

10 So, ye men of intelligence, listen.
   Far be it from God to do evil,
   And from the Almighty to err.
11 For the work of each man He requiteth ;
   He bringeth his way back upon him.

Job

12 God assuredly cannot do wrong.
  The Almighty would not pervert justice.
13 Who entrusted the earth to His charge?
  And who watcheth over the universe?
14 If He should recall His spirit
  And gather His breath to Himself,
15 All flesh together would perish,
  And man would return to the dust.

16 If thou art wise, listen to this,
  And give ear to the sound of my words.
17 Could One rule to whom justice were odious?
  Condemn'st thou the Just and the Mighty One,
18 Who saith to a king, " Thou villain ! "
  To nobles, " Ye infamous men ! "—
19 Who showeth no favour to princes,
  Regardeth not rich more than poor?
  For the work of His hands are they all:
20   In a moment they die—at midnight.
  The rich[2] are convulsed, they pass:
  He mysteriously[3] removeth the mighty.
21 For His eyes are over man's ways,
  Every one of his steps He beholdeth.
22 No darkness is there and no gloom
  Where the workers of wrong may be hidden.
23 No time doth He set for man
  To appear before God in judgment:[4]
24 He shatters the strong without trial,
  And others He sets in their place.
25 For He giveth heed to their works;
  In the night He doth overturn them.
26 Beneath their crimes they are crushed;
  He smites them in presence of witnesses;

The Wisdom Books

27 For they turned from following Him,
    And they gave no heed to His ways.
28 So the crushed were driven to cry to Him,
    And the call of the wretched He heard.
29 But if *He* remain silent, who then can condemn Him?
    If He hide His face, who can bring Him to task?
    Yet He watches o'er nations and men,
30   That none reigns who would wrong the people.[5]
31 Say to God, " I have borne my sin,
    I will not offend any more.
32 Now I see it : O teach me Thyself.
    Have I sinned ? I will do so no more."
33 Must He recompense after *thy* wishes,
    That thou hast rejected (His ways) ?
    'Tis for thee to decide—not for me ;[6]
    Then utter the thing that thou knowest.
34 Men of intellect will admit—
    Men of wisdom who listen to me—
35 That Job hath not spoken with knowledge,
    His words are not marked by insight.
36 O that Job might be tried to the end
    For the wickedness of his answers ![7]
37 For he addeth rebellion to sin,[8]
    And multiplies words against God.

XXXV.
1   Then Elihu went on :
2 Thinkest thou this to be just,
    Dost thou call it thy right before God,
3 To ask, " What advantage is mine ?
    What the better am I, if I sin not ? " ?
4 Well, I will give thee an answer,
    And thy three friends as well.

Job

5 Look to the heavens and see,
   And observe the clouds high overhead.
6 What effect hath thy sin upon Him ?
   What cares He for thy many transgressions ?
7 What gain comes to Him from thy righteousness ?
   What receives He from thy hand ?
8 'Tis to men like thyself thy sin matters,
   'Tis mortals thy righteousness touches.
9 Under sore oppression men cry
   For help from the arm of the tyrant ;
10 But none saith, " Where is God my Creator ? " ¹⎯
   The Giver of songs in the night,
11 Who grants us more knowledge than beasts,
   And more wisdom than birds of the air.
12 Then they cry, but receive no answer,
   Because of their impious pride.²
13 For to idle cries God will not listen,
   Nor will the Almighty regard them.
14 And when He seems not to regard thee,
   Be still and wait patiently for Him.
15 But now that His wrath doth not punish,
   And sin He not greatly regardeth,
16 Job opens his mouth thus idly,
   And poureth forth words without knowledge.

God's Disciplinary Methods Illustrated in History

xxxvi.
1   Then Elihu continued :
2 Wait, I pray, but a while ; I will show thee :
   I have yet to say somewhat for God.
3 With knowledge fetched from afar
   I will justify my Creator.
4 For truly my words are no lie ;
   One in knowledge complete stands before thee.

87

The Wisdom Books

5 Behold, God spurneth the stubborn,[1]
6   The wicked He spareth not :
    But He granteth the rights of the wretched,
7   Withdraws not their due from the just.
    It has happened to kings on the throne,
      Seated in pride and glory,
8 That prisoners in chains they became,
      Held fast in the cords of misery :
9 Then He set forth before them their doings,
      Their proud and rebellious behaviour ;
10 He opened their ears to instruction
      And bade them turn back from sin.
11 If they hearken and do Him homage,
      They finish their days in prosperity.[2]
12 But if stubborn, they pass to Sheol,
      They die without coming to knowledge.
13 For, godless at heart, they grow sullen ;
      They cry not for help when He binds them.
14 They die in the days of their youth,
      Like sodomites they perish.
15 The sufferer He saveth through suffering ;
      Adversity opens his ear.

16 But thou hast been lured by thy freedom,
      By ease at the jaws of distress,
    By the fat on thy well-filled table,
      And the absence of trouble to haunt thee.[3]
17 The full fate of the wicked is thine ;
      Thou art held in the grasp of His judgment.
18 Let[4] not chastisement make thee resentful,
      Nor let the high ransom deflect thee.[5]
19 Wouldst thou marshal thy plaint against Him,
      And all the resource of thy might ?

Job

20 Let not folly beguile thee to rival
   The man who doth think himself wise.[6]
21 Beware, and incline not to sin,
   Nor make choice of sin rather than suffering.

God's Marvellous Ways in Nature

22 See! God by His power doeth loftily—
   Who is a teacher like Him?
23 Who hath enjoined Him His way?
   Or who hath said, " Thou doest wrongly "?
24 Remember to magnify Him
   For His work, whereof men have sung.
25 All men look with pleasure thereon,
   Though man seeth it but from afar.
26 Behold! God is great beyond knowledge,
   The tale of His years beyond search.
27 For He draweth up drops from the sea,
   Which He poureth in rain from His vapour,
28 Wherewith, as the clouds distil,
   They drop down in showers upon men.
29 Who can tell how the clouds are spread out,
   How He thunders from His pavilion?
30 He spreadeth His vapour[7] around Him;
   He covers the tops of the mountains.
31 Therewith He sustaineth[8] the nations,
   And food in abundance He giveth.
32 He wrappeth His hands in the lightning,
   And biddeth it fly to its mark.
33 His thunder announces His coming;
   His anger is kindled at wrong.[9]

xxxvii.

1 At this doth thy heart not tremble,
  And leap right out of its place?

The Wisdom Books

2 Hark, hark to His voice tempestuous,
  To the roar that goes forth from His mouth.
3 'Neath the whole sky He letteth it loose,
  And His flash to the fringe of the world.
4 In the wake of it roareth His voice,
  With His voice majestic He thunders;
  Nor holds He the lightnings back,
  Whensoever His voice is heard.

5 God letteth us see[1] His wonders;
  Great things beyond knowledge He doeth.
6 For He saith to the snow, "Fall earthwards";
  Likewise to His strong rushing rain.
7 He sealeth up all mankind,[2]
  That His work may be known of them all.
8 The beasts go into their lairs,
  And within their dens remain.
9 The tempest comes out of its chamber,
  And out of its store-house the cold.
10 By the breath of God ice is given,
  The broad waters lie in constraint.
11 Yea, He ladeth the thick cloud with hail,
  And the cloud doth scatter His lightning.
12 This way and that it darteth,
  Turning about by His guidance,
  Doing whate'er He commands it
  Over the face of His world,
13 Whether for curse and correction
  Or in mercy He sendeth it forth.[3]

14 Hearken to this, Job, stand still,
  And consider the wonders of God.
15 Dost thou know how God doeth His work;
  How He flashes the light of His cloud?

Job

16 Dost thou know how the thick clouds are poised;
 How He pours down a flood when it thunders,[4]
17 What time thy garments grow hot
 From the south wind which laps earth in silence?
18 Like Him canst thou spread out the sky,
 Which is strong as a molten mirror?

19 How then shall we speak to Him? Tell me;
 For helpless are we in our darkness.
20 Shall one cavil at Him when He speaketh?[5]
 Or shall a man say that He errs?
21 Now no man can look on the light,
 So dazzling bright in the sky,
 When the wind has passed over and cleared it,
22 And radiance comes out of the north;
 But the splendour of God—how terrible!
23 The Almighty we cannot find out.
 Powerful is He and all-righteous,
 And justice He will not pervert.
24 For this cause ought mortals to fear Him:
 But the heart of conceit He despiseth.

THE MYSTERY OF THE DIVINE WISDOM
(xxviii)[1]
(As for Wisdom—whence cometh she?
Understanding—where hath she her home?)
1 For[2] a mine there is for the silver,
   And a place where the gold is refined.
2 Iron is taken from dust,
   And copper is smelted from stone.
3 Man explores the dark to its limits,
   Seeks stones from the blackest gloom.[3]
4 He breaketh a shaft through the ground :
   Forgotten, they hang without foothold ;
   They swing to and fro far from men.[4]
5 From the surface of earth cometh bread,
   While, beneath, it is raked as by fire.
6 Her stones are the home of the sapphire ;
   The dust thereof is gold.
9 He puts forth his hand on the rock ;
   At their roots he o'erturneth the mountains.
10a Channels he cuts in the rocks,
11a   And he bindeth the streams that they weep not.
10b Each precious thing his eye seeth ;
11b   He bringeth the secret to light.

12 *But Wisdom—whence cometh she ?*
   Understanding—where hath she her home ?
7 The pathway is strange to the vulture,
   Unseen by the eye of the hawk,
8 By the sons of pride [5] untrodden,
   Nor ever by fierce lion skirted.
13 The way to her no man knoweth ;
   In the land of the living none finds her.

Job

14 The deep saith, " She is not in me ";
    And the sea saith, " She is not in me."
15 No fine gold for her can be given,
    Nor silver be paid as her price.
16 Not in Ophir gold can she be valued,
    In precious onyx or sapphire.
17 Gold and clear glass are no match for her,
    Jewels of gold no exchange for her.
18 Speak not of coral or crystal ;
    More precious than rubies is Wisdom.
19 The topaz of Cush[6] is no match for her,
    In pure gold she cannot be valued.

20 *But Wisdom—whence cometh she ?*
    Understanding—where hath she her home ?
21 She is hid from the eyes of all living,
    Concealed from the birds of the air.
22 Abaddon[7] and Death declare,
    " A rumour of her we have heard."
23 But the way to her God understandeth,
    And He alone knoweth her home.
24 For He looks to the ends of the earth
    And all things under heaven He beholds.
25 When He settled the weight of the wind
    And meted the waters by measure,
26 Created a law for the rain,
    And a path for the flash of the lightning,
27 Even then did He see and declare her,
    Establish and search her out.
28 And He said unto man, " Behold !
    The fear of Me—that is Wisdom,
    And turning from wrong—Understanding."

TWO WONDERFUL CREATURES OF GOD

The Hippopotamus (xl. 15—24)

15 Behold[1] now the huge beast[2] beside thee :
   He eateth up grass like an ox.
16 Behold now the strength in his loins,
   And the force in the muscles of his belly.
17 He holds his tail stiff as a cedar,
   His thighs are of sinews entwined.
18 His bones are as tubes of brass,
   His limbs are like bars of iron.
19 He is chief of the ways of God,
   Made to lord it over his fellows.[3]
20 The mountains yield him their fruits ;
   All the wild beasts he grindeth to powder.[4]
21 There under the lotus he lies,
   In the covert of reed and fen,
22 Protected by shade of the lotus,
   Encircled by water-willows.
23 From the wild rushing torrent he flees not ;
   He is calm in the swell of a Jordan.
24 Who would venture to make for his eyes,
   Or to pierce through his nose with a cord ?

The Crocodile (xli.)

1 Canst thou draw out the crocodile[1] with hook,
  Or press his tongue down with a cord ?
2 Canst thou put a rope into his nose,
  Or pierce his jaws through with a hook ?

Job

3 Will he make many prayers unto thee,
   Or will he speak softly to thee ?
4 Will he make any tryst with thee,
   To be kept as thy servant for ever ?
5 Wilt thou play with him as with a bird,
   Or attach him to string for thy maidens ?
6 Shall the (fisher) guilds traffic in him ?
   Shall the merchants divide him in pieces ?
7 Canst thou fill his skin with barbs,
   Or his head with the fish-harpoon ?
8 Lay but thine hand upon him :
   Remember the battle—enough !
9 See ! thy hope[2] is but an illusion ;
   God hurleth the dread of him far.
10 Not one is so bold as to rouse him ;
   Where is he that can stand before him ?
11 Who hath ever triumphantly braved him ?
   Beneath the whole heaven, not one.

12 Of his limbs I[3] will not keep silence,
   Of his strength and his mighty equipment.
13 Who can lay bare the face of his garment,
   Or enter the folds of his breastplate ?
14 Who can open the doors of his face ?
   Round about his teeth lieth terror.
15 His back is a ripple of shields,
   And his breast is a seal of flint.
16 One shield is so near to another
   That no air can come between them.
17 Each cleaveth so close to his fellow,
   So locked, that they cannot be severed.
18 Through the breath of his nostrils light flashes,
   His eyes are the lids of the morning.

The Wisdom Books

19 Out of his mouth go torches
  And sparks of fire leap forth.
20 Smoke issues out of his nostrils,
  Like a seething and boiling pot.
21 His breath setteth coals ablaze,
  And a flame goeth forth from his mouth.
22 His neck is the home of strength,
  And terror danceth before him.
23 The flakes of his flesh are welded
  So firm that they cannot be moved.
24 His heart is as firm as a stone—
  Yea, firm as the nether mill-stone.
25 When he lifts himself, strong men are terrified ;
  At his teeth are the mighty dismayed.[4]
26 No sword availeth against him,
  Nor spear nor dart nor arrow.
27 He counteth iron as straw,
  And brass as rotten wood ;
28 No arrow can put him to flight ;
  On him sling-stones are turned to stubble.
29 Clubs are counted as reed,
  And he laughs at the whirr of a javelin.
30 Beneath him (his scales, like) sharp sherds
  Spread marks, as of sledge, on the mire.
31 He makes the deep boil like a pot ;
  He stirreth the sea like ointment.
32 In his wake is a shining path—
  One would think the deep to be hoary.
33 There is not his like upon earth,
  Created to know no fear.[5]
34 Everything that is high is afraid of him :[6]
  He is king o'er the sons of pride.[7]

PROVERBS

ON THE WORTH OF WISDOM (Proverbs i.—ix.)

i.
1 The proverbs of Solomon, the son of David, king of Israel.

The Aim of the Book

2 That men may learn wisdom and discipline,
  And understand words of discernment ;
3 That they may win training in prudence,
  In right and in justice and rectitude ;
4 That shrewdness be imparted to the simple,
  And knowledge and insight to youth—
5 The wise too, who listens, will grow wiser,
  And the prudent more skilled in direction—
6 That proverbs and parables may be plain,
  Even the words of the wise and their riddles

The Motto of the Book

7 The fear of the Lord is the basis[1] of knowledge,
  But wisdom and discipline are scorned of fools.

Exhortation and Warning

8 Hearken, my son, to thy father's instruction,
  And do not forsake what thy mother hath taught thee ;
9 For a chaplet of grace shall they[2] be to thy head,
  And a chain for thy neck.

10 My son, if sinners entice thee,
11   Consent thou not. If they say,

The Wisdom Books

"Come with us, let us lurk for the blameless,[3]
And wantonly ambush the innocent—
12 Let us swallow them up like the grave,[4] alive
And entire, even as those that go down to the pit.
13 Precious wealth of all sorts shall be ours;
We shall fill our houses with spoil.
14 Do but cast in thy lot with us;
We shall all of us have but one purse,"
15 Go[5] not in the way with them,
Keep thy foot away from their path;
17 For[6] the net is spread in vain
In the sight of a thing that hath wings.
18 Their own is the blood that they lurk for,
Their own are the lives that they ambush.
19 Thus end all who would grasp at gain—
It destroyeth the life of its owner.

The Appeal of Wisdom

20 Wisdom crieth aloud in the streets,
In the squares doth she utter her voice,
21 From the top of the walls[7] she calleth,
At the doors of the gate-ways she saith,
22 "How long will ye foolish love folly,
And scoffers delight them in scoffing,
And fools in their hatred of knowledge?
23 O turn ye to my reproof.
See! I utter my mind[8] unto you;
I will tell you what I have determined.
24 Because ye refused my call,
Gave no heed to my hand when it beckoned you,
25 But rejected all my counsel,
And refused mine admonition,

Proverbs

26 When distress falls on you, *I* will laugh ;
   I will mock, when your terror cometh,
27 When your terror doth come as a storm,
   As a whirlwind your distress.[9]
28 Then I will not answer their call ;
   They may seek, but they shall not find me.
29 Because they hated knowledge,
   And rejected the fear of the Lord,
30 Would nothing of my counsel,
   But despised all mine admonition,
31 They must eat the fruit of their ways,
   And be filled with their own devices.
32 By their own self-will[10] shall the simple be slain,
   And prosperous ease shall bring fools to destruction.
33 But secure shall he dwell that listens to me,
   In a peace unruffled by fear of calamity."

The Blessed Fruits of Wisdom

ii.
1 My son, if thou welcome my words,
   And lay up with thee my commandments,
2 Giving heedful ear unto wisdom,
   And bending thy mind unto reason ;
3 If thou wilt invoke understanding,
   And lift up thy voice unto reason,
4 Seeking for her as for silver,
   And searching for her as for treasure :
5 Then the fear of the Lord shall be plain to thee,
   And the knowledge of God thou shalt find.
6 For the Lord is the Giver of wisdom,
   The Source[1] of knowledge and insight.
7 For the upright He layeth up deliverance ;
   He shieldeth the blameless life.

The Wisdom Books

8   He guardeth the paths of the just,
    And the way of the faithful He watcheth.
9   Then justice and right shall be plain to thee;
    Thou wilt keep² to all paths that are good.

10 When wisdom shall enter thy mind,
    And in knowledge thou findest thy pleasure,
11 Discretion shall watch over thee,
    And understanding shall guard thee,
12 And save thee from wicked ways,
    From men of perverse speech,
13 Who leave the paths of right,
    To walk in ways of darkness—
14 Happy in doing wrong,
    Exulting in wicked perverseness,
15 All crooked in their paths,
    And devious in their ways.

16 From the lewd³ woman⁴ too, it⁵ shall save thee,
    The harlot of slippery speech,
17 Who forsaketh the friend of her youth,⁶
    And forgetteth her bond with her God;
18 For her house sinketh down to death,
    And her paths lead straight to the Shades.
19 None that visit her ever come back,
    Or arrive at the paths of life.
20 Therefore⁷ walk in the way of good men,
    And keep in the paths of the righteous,
21 For the upright shall dwell in the land,
    And the blameless alone shall enjoy it;
22 While bad men from it shall be severed,
    And faithless men rooted away.

Proverbs

The Wisdom of Trusting and Honouring the Lord

iii.
1. My son, forget not my teaching,
   But keep my commandments in mind;
2. For a long and happy life[1]
   And fulness of peace[2] will they bring thee.
3. Let not kindness and faithfulness leave thee,
   Bind them about thy neck;[3]
4. So favour and good repute[4] shalt thou find
   Alike with God and man.
5. Trust the Lord with all thy heart,
   Lean not on thine own understanding:
6. In all thy ways acknowledge Him,
   And He will smooth thy paths.
7. Do not plume thyself on thy wisdom;
   Fear the Lord and turn from evil;
8. Then there will be health to thy body,[5]
   And refreshment to thy bones.
9. If thou honour the Lord with thy wealth,
   With the first-fruits of all that comes in to thee,
10. Thy barns shall be filled with corn,[6]
    And with wine shall thy vats overflow.

The Worth of Wisdom

11. Reject not, my son, the Lord's chastening,
    And do not spurn[7] His reproof;
12. For whom the Lord loveth He chasteneth,
    And the son He delights in He paineth.[8]
13. Happy the man that finds wisdom,
    The man that obtains understanding;
14. For she brings a gain fairer than silver,
    A revenue better than gold.

The Wisdom Books

15 More precious is she than corals,
   And with her can no treasures compare.
16 In her right hand is length of days,
   In her left are riches and honour.
17 Her ways are pleasant ways,
   And all her paths are peace.
18 She is life[9] unto those that grasp her ;
   Happy they that hold her fast.

19 The Lord by wisdom founded the earth,
   By understanding established the heavens.
20 By knowledge He broke up the deeps,
   And the clouds He made drip with dew.

The Security that comes from Wisdom

21b Observe, my son, discretion and wisdom,
21a   Let them never out of thy sight ;
22 So shall they be life unto thee,
   An ornament round thy neck.
23 Thou shalt then go thy way securely,
   Without ever striking thy foot.[10]
24 Thou shalt sit down[11] unafraid,
   And thy sleep shall be sweet where thou liest.
25 Thou shalt fear no sudden terror,[12]
   Nor the tempest that falls on the wicked ;
26 For the Lord is the ground of thy hope ;
   He will keep thy foot from the snare.

27 Withhold from thy neighbour[13] no good
   Which thou hast in thy power to do him.
28 Do not tell him—when thou canst afford it—to go
   And come back, with the promise of something
      to-morrow.

Proverbs

29 Devise no mischief against thy neighbour,
   While he is trustfully dwelling beside thee.
30 Do not idly quarrel with a man
   Who has not done thee any harm.

31 Do not envy the violent man,
   Or choose any one of his ways;
32 For the Lord abhorreth the crooked,
   But the upright are His friends.
33 The Lord's curse rests on the house of the wicked,
   But the home of the righteous He blesseth.
34 As for Him, He scoffeth at scoffers,
   But He giveth grace to the lowly.
35 Wise men come to honour,
   But shame is the portion of fools.

The Excellence and Beneficent Power of Wisdom

iv.
1 Listen, children, to a father's instruction;
  Give heed to acquaint you with understanding.
2 For good is the counsel I give unto you;
  Forsake ye not my teaching.

3 When I was my father's child,
  Beloved of my mother, and tender,
4 He used to say, as he taught me,
  "Hold fast my words in thy mind.
  Keep my commandments and live;
5   Get wisdom, get understanding.[1]
6 If thou leave her not, she will keep thee;
  If thou hold her dear, she will guard thee.[2]
8 Prize her, and she will exalt thee
  And honour thee, if thou embrace her.

9   She will set a fair wreath on thy head,
     And a glorious crown she will give thee."
10 Listen, my son, and accept my words,
     And the years of thy life shall be many.
11 I teach thee the way of wisdom,
     I guide thee in honour's paths.
12 Thou shalt walk with steps unconstrained,
     Thou shalt run without ever stumbling.
13 Keep unceasing hold of instruction;[3]
     Guard her, for she is thy life.
14 Enter not on the path of the wicked;
     Walk not in the way of the evil.
15 Pass over it not, but avoid it;
     Turn thee aside, and pass on.
16 For they sleep not unless they have done some harm;
     They are sleepless until they have wrought some ruin.
17 For the bread that they eat is won by crime,
     And the wine that they drink is procured by cruelty.[4]
19 The way of the wicked is through[5] deep darkness,
     Which hideth from them whereat they stumble;
18 But the way of the just is like light of the morning,
     Which shines more and more till the day is full.
20 My son, give heed to my words;
     Bend thine ear to the things that I say.
21 Let them not away from thy sight,
     But keep them within thy heart:
22 They are life unto those that find them,
     And health to all their being.
23 Guard thy heart with all vigilance,
     For this is the way to life.[6]

Proverbs

24 Put away from thee crooked speech,
   And banish all devious talk.
25 Let thine eyes look straight in front,
   And thine eyelids right before thee.
26 Make a level path for thy feet,
   And let all thy ways be firm.
27 Turn not to the right or the left;
   Keep thy foot away from evil.

The Wrong and Folly of Impurity
The Deadly Power of an Evil Woman

v.
1 My son, give heed unto wisdom,
   Bend thine ear to understanding;
2 That discretion may watch over thee,
   And that knowledge may preserve thee.[1]
3 For the lips of the harlot[2] drop honey,
   Her mouth is smoother than oil;
4 But at last she is bitter as wormwood,
   And sharp as a two-edged sword.
5 Her feet go down to Death;
   Her steps lead straight into Sheol.
6 No smooth way of life walks she;
   Her paths wander—she knoweth not whither.[3]

7 And now, my son,[4] listen to me;
   Turn not from the words that I utter.
8 Move far away from her,
   Come not nigh the door of her house;
9 Lest thou give thy wealth[5] unto others,
   Thy years[6] unto the implacable,[7]
10 And so strangers enjoy thy substance,
   And a family of aliens thy toil;
11 And thus at the last thou groanest,[8]
   When body and flesh are consumed:

12 " O why did I hate instruction,
   And spurn reproof in my heart ?
13 Why listened I not to my teachers,
   Nor bent to instructors mine ear ?
14 All but utterly was I undone
   In the congregation assembled."[*]

Exhortation to Fidelity

15 Drink water from thine own cistern,
   Running water from thine own well.
16 Let thy springs not[10] be scattered abroad,
   On the streets thy streams of water.
17 Let them be for thyself alone,
   And not for strangers beside thee.
18 Let thy fountain be thine own,[11]
   Get thee joy from the wife of thy youth—
19   Lovely hind and graceful doe—
   Let her breasts make thee happy[12] at all times,
   With her love be thou ravished for ever.
20 For why with a stranger[13] be ravished,
   And an alien's[13] bosom embrace ?
21 For the ways of a man are before the Lord's eyes,
   And all his paths He weigheth.
22 His iniquities shall snare him,
   Enmeshed in the toils of his sin.
23 He shall die for lack of instruction,
   And perish for his vast folly.

Warning against the Adulteress

vi.
20* Observe,[1] my son, the commands of thy father,
   And do not abandon thy mother's instruction.

[*] For vi. 1—19, see pp. 115—117.

Proverbs

21 Bind them upon thy heart for ever ;
   Hang them round about thy neck.
22 When thou walkest, Wisdom[2] will guide thee ;
   When thou liest down, she will watch thee ;
   When thou wakest up, she will talk with thee.
23 For precept illumines, instruction enlightens,
   And reproof that disciplines leads unto life,
24 Preserving thee safe from the wife of another,[3]
   From the slippery tongue of the stranger.

25 Do not long in thy heart for her beauty,
   And do not be caught by her eyes.
26 For, while harlotry costs but a morsel of bread,[4]
   'Tis the precious life the adulteress[5] hunteth.
27 Can a man take fire in his bosom
   Without his clothes being burned ?
28 Or on glowing coals can he walk
   Without his feet being scorched ?
29 So with him that approacheth his neighbour's wife :
   None that toucheth her ever may go unpunished.
30 Do men not[6] despise a thief,
   When he steals even to satisfy hunger ?
31 When caught, he must[7] pay seven-fold,
   And give all that his house contains.
32 But the adulterer is witless :
   He destroyeth himself by his doings.
33 For stripes and disgrace will be his,
   And a shame that will never be blotted.
34 For jealousy maddens a man ;
   In the day of revenge he is pitiless.
35 No ransom will he accept,
   Nor will gifts in profusion content him.

The Wisdom Books

Another Warning

vii.
1 My son, observe my words,
    And lay up with thee my commandments.
2 Keep my commandments and live,
    And my teaching as the pupil of thine eye.
3 Bind them upon thy fingers;
    Write them on the tablet of thy heart.
4 Say to Wisdom, " Thou art my sister ";
    Call Understanding thy friend—
5 That thou shun the dissolute woman,
    The stranger of slippery speech.

6 At the window of her[1] house
    She[1] peers out through the lattice;
7 And, looking at the simpletons,
    She detects a silly youth,
8 As he passes near the street corner,
    Stepping the way to her house,
9 Just in the evening twilight,
    As the night is growing dark.
10 See! the woman comes out to meet him,
    In a harlot's dress, all a-flutter.[2]
11 Boisterous and brazen[3] is she:
    Her feet are restless at home.
12 Now in street, now in square is she,
    Lurking near every corner.
13 So she catches and kisses him,
    And with impudent face she accosts him:
14 " I have ready a thanksgiving feast,[4]
    For to-day I have paid my vows;
15 And so I came out to meet thee,
    To seek thee, and now I have found thee.

Proverbs

16 I have spread my couch with coverlets,
   Striped with Egyptian yarn.
17 I have perfumed my bed with myrrh,
   With cinnamon and with aloes.
18 Come; let us drink love till the morning,
   And yield us to merry caresses.
19 For my husband[5] is not at home;
   He is far away on a journey.
20 He has taken a money-bag with him,
   He will not come home till full moon."
21 With her much fair speech she beguiled him,
   With her blandishing words she enticed him.
22 So he followed her bewitched,[6]
   Like an ox that is brought to the slaughter,
   Like a dog that is led on a chain,[7]
23b Like a bird rushing into a net,
23c Unaware that its life is at stake,
23a Till an arrow pierces its liver.

24 And now, my son,[8] listen to me,
   And give heed to the words that I utter.
25 Let thy heart not swerve to her ways,
   And wander not in her paths;
26 For the dead she hath cast down are many,
   And many are those she hath slain.
27 Her house is the road to Sheol,
   Straight down to the chambers of Death.

The Invitation and the Rewards of Wisdom
viii. *Wisdom's Appeal to Men*
1 Hark! for Wisdom is calling,
   And Reason is lifting her voice:
2 On a raised place, high by the way,
   On the streets she hath taken her stand.

The Wisdom Books

3 By the gates that lead into the city,
   She crieth aloud at the portals:[1]
4 " Unto you, O men, I call,
   And my voice is to all mankind.
5 Ye simple ones, learn to be prudent ;
   Ye foolish ones, get to know wisdom.
6 O listen, for grave[2] is my message,
   And right all the speech of my lips.
7 It is truth that my mouth discourses,
   And falsehood[3] my lips abhor.
8 All the words that I utter are honest,
   Free from all that is crooked and tortuous,
9 All clear[4] to the man of sense,
   And right unto those that have knowledge.
10 Choose instruction, then, rather than silver,
   And more than choice gold welcome knowledge.
11 For better is Wisdom than corals;
   No treasures with her can compare.
12 I, Wisdom, possess[5] intelligence ;
   Knowledge and insight are mine.
14 Mine[6] are counsel and skill ;
   Understanding and might are mine.
15 By me do monarchs reign
   And rulers administer justice.
16 By me do princes govern
   And noblemen rule[7] the earth.
17 Those that love me I love,
   And those that seek me find me.
18 With me are riches and honour,
   Prosperity and grandeur.[8]
19 My fruit is better than finest gold,
   My revenue fairer than choicest silver.

20 I walk in the way that is fair,[9]
    And keep to the paths of justice,
21 Endowing with wealth those that love me,
    And filling their treasuries full.

Wisdom's Ancient Origin

22 At the very beginning[10] God fashioned[11] me,
    As the first of His works of old.
23 In the ancient time was I formed,
    At the first, when the world began.
24 I was born when as yet no depths were,
    No fountains laden with water;
25 Ere yet the mountains were sunk,
    And before the hills was I born;
26 Ere the earth and the fields were created,
    Or the first of the clods of the world.
27 When He set up the heavens, I was there;
    When He vaulted the face of the deep;
28 When He made firm the skies above,
    And fixed the deep fast at its sources;
29 When He set to the sea its bounds,[12]
    As He marked off the base of the world.
30 Then beside Him was I as His nursling,[13]
    And I was His daily delight,
    Playing before Him at all times,
31 Playing about in His world,
    Delighting in humankind.

Wisdom's Concluding Appeal

32 And now, children, listen to me:
    Happy those that keep to my ways.
33 Hear instruction, and thus get ye wisdom.
    Reject not mine admonition.[14]

34 Happy he who listens to me,
    Daily watching at my gates,
    And waiting at my door-posts.
35 For who findeth me findeth life,
    He winneth the Lord's own favour;
36 But who misses me wrongs himself,
    For all that hate me love death.

The Two Hostesses—Wisdom and Folly
The Invitation of Wisdom

ix.
1 Wisdom[1] hath built her a house,
    Hath set up[2] her seven pillars,
2 Slain her beasts, and mingled her wine,
    And also spread her table.
3 She hath sent forth her maidens to cry
    On the thoroughfares of the city:
4 " All simple ones, turn in hither,
    I[3] would speak unto him that lacks wisdom.
5 Come and eat of my bread,
    And drink of the wine I have mingled.
6 Abandon your folly, and live,
    And walk in the way of reason.
11 For by me thy days shall be many,
    And the years of thy life increased." [4]

The Invitation of Folly

13 Dame Folly is loud and seductive,
    A stranger to shame[5] is she.
14 At the door of her house she sitteth,
    On the thoroughfares of the city,
15 Calling to passers-by,
    Who are going straight on their way:

Proverbs

16 "All simple ones, turn in hither,
   I would speak unto him that lacks wisdom.⁶
17 Stolen waters are sweet,
   And bread eaten in secret is pleasant."
18 But he knows not that dead men⁷ are there,
   That her guests lie sunken in Sheol.

A Group of Aphorisms

7 Who⁸ correcteth a scoffer but gets himself insult,
   And a stain⁹ rests on him that reproveth the wicked.
8 Reprove not a scoffer, or else he may hate thee;
   But a wise man reprove, and for that he will love thee.
9 Give¹⁰ to a wise man, and he will grow wiser;
   Instruct the righteous, and more he will learn.
10 The fear of the Lord is the first step to wisdom,¹¹
   And to know the Holy One is understanding.
12 If thou art wise, thou art wise for thyself;
   And if thou dost scoff, thou must bear it¹² alone.

Warnings

Against Suretyship

vi.
1 My son¹, if thou hast gone bail for thy neighbour,
   And given thy pledge for another;
2 If by thine own lips thou art snared,
   And art trapped by the words of thy mouth:
3 Then this do, my son, and free thyself,
   Since thou hast come into his power;
   Go, bestir thee,² besiege thy neighbour;
4 Give no sleep to thine eyes,
   Nor slumber to thine eyelids,

The Wisdom Books

5 Shake thyself free, like a roe, from the snare,³
  Or a bird from the hand of the fowler.

Against Indolence

6 Go to the ant, thou sluggard;
  Consider her ways, and be wise.
7 Without officer, ruler, or chief,
8 She provideth her bread in the summer,
  And gathereth her food in the harvest.

9 How long wilt thou lie, O sluggard?
  When wilt thou rise from thy sleep?
10 "Just⁴ a little more sleep, a little more slumber,
  A little more lying with folded hands."
11 So shall poverty come upon thee like a robber,⁵
  And want like an armed man.

Against Underhand Mischief-making

12 Sunk in wickedness is the man⁶
  Whose speech is ingrained with falsehood—
13 Who winks his eyes,
  Or shuffles⁷ his feet,
  Or makes signs with his fingers,
14 Gives his mind to the planning of mischief,
  And always is scattering discord.
15 For these things shall sudden disaster assail him;
  He shall swiftly be crushed beyond all hope of healing.

Seven Detestable Things

16 Six things there are which the Lord detesteth;
  Yea, seven⁸ doth He abhor:—

Proverbs

17 Haughty eyes, a lying tongue,
    And hands that shed innocent blood,
18 A mind that plans wicked devices,
    And feet that are swift to do wrong,
19 A false witness that uttereth lies,
    One that scattereth strife among brethren.

FIRST COLLECTION OF PROVERBS[1] (x. 1—xxii. 16)

x.
1   The Proverbs of Solomon:

A wise son maketh his father glad,
But a foolish son is a grief to his mother.
2 Treasures wrongly acquired profit nothing,
But righteousness saveth from death.
3 The Lord will not suffer the righteous to hunger,
But He will frustrate the desire of the wicked.
4 A slack hand createth poverty,
But a diligent hand maketh rich.
5 He that gathers in summer acts wisely;
He that sleepeth in harvest acts shamefully.
6 The blessing of God[2] is on the head of the righteous,
But[3] sorrow[4] shall cover the face[5] of the wicked.
7 The memory of the righteous is blessed,
But the name of the wicked shall rot.[6]
8 A wise man gives heed to commands,
But a foolish talker will fall.
9 He whose life is blameless walks safely,
But he who lives crookedly smarts for it.[7]
10 He who winketh the eye[8] maketh trouble,
But frank reproof maketh peace.[9]
11 A fountain of life is the mouth of the righteous,
But the mouth of the wicked is wrapped in violence.
12 Hatred stirreth up strife,
But love hideth all transgressions.
13 On the lips of a prudent man wisdom is found,
But a man without sense needs a rod for his back.[10]

Proverbs

14 Wise men keep what they know to themselves,
   But the mouth of the fool is impending destruction.
15 The rich man's wealth is his fortified city ; [11]
   But the poor, by their poverty, come to destruction.
16 The wage of the righteous conduceth to life,
   But their revenue bringeth the wicked to ruin.[12]
17 The way to life is to heed instruction,
   But to turn from reproof is to go astray.
18 Righteous[13] lips cover up hatred,
   But the slanderer is a fool.
19 Where words are many, offences are certain ;
   But he that controlleth his tongue doeth wisely.
20 The tongue of the just is like choicest silver,
   But the mind of the wicked is little worth.
21 The speech of the righteous is sustenance to many,
   But lack of sense is the death of fools.
22 It is only the blessing of God that brings wealth,
   And He addeth no sorrow therewith.
23 To a fool the doing of wrong is as sport,
   But a man of sense abhors[14] it.
24 What the wicked feared shall befall him,
   But the desire of the righteous shall be granted.
25 When the whirlwind passeth, the wicked shall vanish,
   But the righteous is firmly established for ever.
26 As vinegar to the teeth, and as smoke to the eyes,
   Even so is the sluggard to them that send him.
27 The fear of the Lord prolongs life,
   But the years of the wicked are shortened.
28 The hope of the righteous shall end in gladness,
   But the wicked shall fail of their expectation.

The Wisdom Books

29 To the man that is blameless the Lord is a stronghold,
   But terror and ruin to those that do evil.
30 The righteous shall be unmoved for ever,
   But the wicked shall have no home in the land.
31 The mouth of the righteous bringeth forth wisdom,
   But the man of false tongue shall be rooted out.
32 The lips of the righteous utter[15] good-will;
   But the mouth of the wicked, malice.

xi.
1 The Lord detests a false balance,[1]
   But a just weight is His delight.
2 Pride is sure to be followed by shame,
   But modesty is wisdom.
3 Their integrity guideth the upright,
   But the false are destroyed by their crookedness.
4 In the day of wrath[2] riches are useless,
   But righteousness saveth from death.
5 The path of the blameless is smoothed by his righteousness,
   But the wicked shall fall by his wickedness.
6 The upright are saved by their righteousness,
   But the false are caught in their evil desires.
7 When a wicked man dies, his hope perishes—[3]
   Yea, the hope of the godless perishes.
8 The righteous is rescued from trouble,
   And the wicked taketh his place.[4]
9 By slander the godless would ruin his neighbour,
   But the righteous are rescued by knowledge.
10 When the righteous flourish, the city rejoiceth;
    When the wicked perish, there is jubilation.
11 By the blessing of the upright, the city is exalted;
    By the mouth of the wicked it is overthrown.

Proverbs

12 A man has no sense that despises his neighbour;
   A man of prudence holds his tongue.
13 Who carries tales divulges secrets,
   But a trustworthy man concealeth a matter.
14 Where guidance is lacking, a people must fall;
   But that people[5] is safe that is rich in counsellors.
15 He who goes bail for another will suffer,
   But he who abhors being surety is sure.[6]
16 A gracious woman obtaineth honour,
   (But[7] a throne of dishonour is she who hates justice.
   Indolent men never come to wealth,)
   But riches are won by the men that are diligent.[8]
17 The kind man does good to himself;
   The cruel man injures himself.[9]
18 The gain of the wicked is but an illusion,
   But he that sows righteousness wins the true wages.
19 Devotion to[10] righteousness leadeth to life;
   The pursuit of wickedness endeth in death.
20 The Lord abhorreth the mind that is crooked,
   But those that walk blamelessly are His delight.
21 Most surely[11] the wicked shall not go unpunished,
   But the righteous folk[12] shall escape.
22 Like a golden ring in the snout of a swine
   Is a beautiful woman without discretion.
23 The desire of the righteous will issue in good,
   But the hope of the wicked in wrath.[13]
24 One man is generous, yet grows ever richer;
   Another is mean, yet he only grows poorer.
25 The liberal soul shall be enriched;
   And he that waters, himself shall be watered.

The Wisdom Books

26 He that holds up corn shall be cursed by the people,
   But blessings shall be on his head that sells it.
27 He who aims at the thing that is good shall win[14] favour,
   But ruin shall come upon him that seeks evil.[15]
28 He who trusts in his riches shall wither,[16]
   But like green leaves the righteous shall flourish.
29 He that harmeth his household shall reap the wind,
   And the fool shall be slave to the man of wisdom.
30 Life[17] is the fruit of righteousness,[18]
   But rapine destroyeth men's lives.[19]
31 If the righteous are punished on earth,
   How much more the sinful and wicked!

xii.
1 He who loves knowledge loves discipline,
   But he that hateth reproof is a boor.
2 A good man winneth the Lord's good-will,
   But a man of evil designs He condemns.
3 By wickedness no man can stand for ever,
   But the root of the righteous remains unmoved.
4 A worthy wife is a crown to her husband,
   But one that brings shame is as rot in his bones.
5 The aims of the righteous are just;
   The designs of the wicked are treacherous.
6 The words of the wicked lurk for blood,[1]
   But the speech of the upright delivers.[2]
7 The wicked shall be overthrown and vanish,
   But the house of the righteous shall stand.
8 A man is commended according to his insight,
   But a wrong-headed man is despised.
9 Better a man of no rank, with a servant,[3]
   Than one who apes greatness and yet has no bread.

Proverbs

10 A righteous man cares for the life of his beast,
 But the heart[4] of the wicked is cruel.
11 He that tilleth his land shall have plenty of bread,
 But he that pursues empty aims shall have none.[5]
12 The wicked is snared by his wickedness,[6]
 But the root of the righteous endures.[7]
13 By the sin of his lips is the wicked ensnared,
 But the righteous escapeth from trouble.
14 The words of a man bring forth good[8] fruit in plenty,
 And the deeds of his hands shall come back upon him.
15 A fool is certain his way is right,
 But a wise man listens to counsel.
16 A fool displays his anger at once,[9]
 But a prudent man hides an affront.
17 One who speaks out the truth affirms justice,
 But a false witness uttereth lies.
18 The chatter of some is like sword-thrusts,
 But the tongue of the wise is healing.
19 The man who speaks truth stands for ever,
 But the false tongue is but for a moment.
20 Hearts of deceit have the men who plan evil,
 But happy are those who plan other men's good.
21 No evil thing can befall the righteous,
 But the wicked are full of misfortune.
22 The Lord abhorreth lying lips,
 But delighteth in those that deal faithfully.
23 A man of prudence conceals what he knows,
 But a fool shouts his folly aloud.
24 The diligent cometh to power,
 But the slothful becometh a serf.
25 Care boweth down a man's heart,
 But a good word maketh it glad.

The Wisdom Books

26 The righteous departeth from evil,[10]
    But the way of the wicked is error.
27 The indolent man will not hunt[11] his game,
    But the diligent man winneth precious[12] wealth.
28 In the path of righteousness there is life,
    But the way of wickedness leads unto death.[13]

xiii.
1 A wise son loveth[1] instruction,
    But a scorner listens not to rebuke.
2 A good man enjoyeth[2] the fruits of his speech,
    But the false are greedy for rapine.
3 He that guardeth his mouth preserveth his life,
    But a wide open mouth brings a man to ruin.
4 The sluggard desireth and hath not,
    But the diligent is enriched.[3]
5 A righteous man hateth deception,
    But the wicked act basely and shamefully.
6 Righteousness guardeth the man of integrity,
    But sin overturneth the wicked.[4]
7 Some pretend to be rich, and have nothing at all;
    Some pretend to be poor, and are rolling in wealth.
8 A man's riches may ransom his life,
    But a poor man listens not to rebuke.[5]
9 The light of the righteous shines on,[6]
    But the lamp of the wicked goes out.
10 Pride causes nothing but strife,
    But with those that take counsel[7] is wisdom.
11 Wealth gathered in haste[8] shall diminish,
    But amassed by degrees it will grow.
12 Hope deferred maketh sick the heart,
    But a wish fulfilled is life.[9]
13 He who scorns the word[10] shall perish,
    But who fears the commandment is safe.[11]

Proverbs

14 The teaching of the wise is a fountain of life,
Whereby to avoid the snares of death.[12]
15 Fine intelligence winneth favour,
But the way of the false is their ruin.[13]
16 The prudent act always with insight,
But the fool flaunteth his folly.
17 An incompetent[14] messenger ruins an enterprise,[15]
But a trustworthy envoy is healing.
18 To reject instruction spells shame and poverty,
But to heed admonition leadeth to honour.
19 Sweet is desire fulfilled,
But fools hate to turn from evil.
20 He that walks with the wise shall be wise,
But the comrade of fools shall smart for it.
21 Sinners are chased by misfortune,
But good overtaketh[16] the righteous.
22 The good man leaves wealth to his children's children,
But the wealth of the sinner is stored for the righteous.
23 The ground of the poor yieldeth food in abundance,
But some by injustice are swept away.[17]
24 He that spareth his rod hateth his son,
But he that loves him chastises him.
25 The righteous, when hungry, may eat their fill,
But the wicked are empty within.

xiv.
1 A wise woman buildeth her house,
But a fool tears it down with her hands.[1]
2 The man who fears God lives honestly,
But the man that is crooked despises Him.
3 The speech of a fool is a rod for his back,[2]
But the words of the wise preserve them

The Wisdom Books

4 Where no oxen are, there can be no³ corn ;
   But plenty of oxen means plenty of produce.
5 A trustworthy witness does not lie,
   But a false witness uttereth lies.
6 A scorner seeks wisdom in vain,
   But to prudent men knowledge is easy.
7 Get thee out of a foolish man's presence,
   For his lips do not utter knowledge.⁴
8 The shrewd show their wisdom by watching their way,
   But the folly of foolish men leads them astray.⁵
9 Guilt has its home among fools,⁶
   But God's favour abides with the upright.
10 The heart knoweth its own bitterness,
   And no stranger can share in its joy.
11 The house of the wicked shall be destroyed,
   But the tent of the upright shall flourish.
12 Many a way seems straight to a man
   Which leads at the last to death.⁷
13 Even in laughter the heart may be sad,
   And the end of joy may be sorrow.
14 He who swerves (from the right) shall pay well for his conduct,
   But the good man shall reap the fruit of his deeds.⁸
15 The simple believe every word,
   But the shrewd look well to their steps.
16 A wise man anxiously shrinketh from evil,
   But a fool plunges into⁹ it jauntily.
17 A man of quick temper acts foolishly,
   But a prudent man is patient.¹⁰
18 The simple come into possession of folly,
   But the wise win the crown of knowledge.

Proverbs

19 The evil must bow before the good,
 And the wicked (crouch down) at the gates of the righteous.
20 The poor man is hated even by his neighbour,
 But the rich hath many friends.
21 He that despiseth his neighbour sinneth,
 But happy is he that doth pity the poor.
22 Surely those that plan evil will stray (to destruction),
 But those that plan good meet with kindness and faithfulness.
23 In all labour there is profit,
 But mere talk tendeth only to penury.
24 The crown of the wise is their wisdom,[11]
 And the garland[12] of fools is their folly.
25 A truthful witness saves life,
 But one that speaks falsely destroys[13] it.
26 He that feareth the Lord hath strong ground of confidence,
 To the children of such He is Refuge.
27 The fear of the Lord is a fountain of life,
 Whereby to avoid the snares of death.[14]
28 Glory falls to the monarch whose people are many,
 But a prince comes to ruin whose people are few.
29 The man of patience shows much good sense,
 But the quick-tempered man shows great folly.
30 A tranquil mind is the life of the body,
 But passion[15] rotteth the bones.
31 He that crusheth the needy revileth his Maker,[16]
 But he that is kind to the poor does Him honour.
32 The wicked is overthrown by his wickedness,
 But the righteous hath a refuge in his integrity.[17]
33 Wisdom dwells in the heart of the prudent,
 But folly[18] in the heart of fools.

The Wisdom Books

34 Righteousness exalteth a nation,
  But sin is a people's disgrace.
35 A competent servant enjoys the king's favour,
  But scandalous service incurs his wrath.

XV.
1 A soft answer turns away wrath,
  But provocative speech stirs up anger.
2 The tongue of the wise droppeth knowledge,
  But the mouth of fools poureth out folly.
3 The eyes of the Lord are everywhere,
  Watching the bad and the good.
4 A soothing tongue is life,[1]
  But violent words break the spirit.
5 A fool despiseth his father's instruction,
  But he that regardeth reproof showeth wisdom.
6 In the house of the righteous is abundance of wealth,
  But the revenue of the wicked is cut off.
7 The lips of the wise disperse knowledge,
  But the mind of fools is unstable.[2]
8 The Lord abhorreth the sacrifice of the wicked,
  But the prayer of the upright He welcomes.
9 The Lord abhorreth the way of the wicked,
  But He loveth the man that is bent upon righteousness.
10 He that leaveth the way shall have discipline sore,
  He that hateth reproof shall die.
11 Before the Lord Sheol and Abaddon[3] lie open;
  How much more the hearts of men!
12 A scoffer loves not reproof,
  He refuses to go with[4] the wise.
13 Joyous heart makes happy face,
  But a sorrowful heart makes a stricken spirit.

Proverbs

14 The mind of the wise seeketh knowledge,
   But the mouth of fools feedeth on folly.
15 To the sad every day is a bad day,
   But an endless feast to the cheerful.
16 Better is little, with the fear of the Lord,
   Than abundance of treasure and trouble therewith.
17 Better a dish of herbs, with love,
   Than a fatted ox, with hatred.
18 An angry man stirreth up strife,
   But a patient man stilleth contention.
19 The way of the sluggard is hedged with thorns,
   But the path of the diligent[5] runs like a highway.
20 A wise son maketh his father glad,[6]
   But a fool of a man despiseth his mother.
21 Folly is joy to a man without sense,
   But a man of good sense is straightforward.
22 Plans are frustrated where there is no counsel;
   But, when many advise, they succeed.[7]
23 Joy comes to the man who makes (happy) retort;[8]
   And a word in season, how good it is!
24 The wise man's path goeth upward[9] to life;
   He avoideth the way to Sheol beneath.
25 The Lord uprooteth the house of the proud,
   But the bounds of the widow He firmly maintaineth.
26 Evil devices the Lord abhorreth,
   But gracious words are His delight.[10]
27 He that is grasping destroys his own house,
   But he that hates presents[11] shall live.
28 Faithfulness[12] broods in the heart of the righteous,
   But evil pours from the mouth of the wicked.
29 The Lord is far from the wicked,
   But the prayer of the righteous He heareth.

30 Shining eyes[13] gladden the heart,
    And good news fattens the bones.
31 He that listens to wholesome reproof [14]
    Shall dwell among the wise.
32 He despiseth himself who rejecteth instruction,
    But he gains understanding who heedeth reproof.
33 The fear of the Lord is instruction in wisdom,
    And honour comes after humility.[15]

xvi.
1 Man may order his thoughts,
   But the word[1] on his tongue is from God.
2 A man's life may seem thoroughly pure to himself,
   But the Lord weigheth the spirit.[2]
3 Commit thy work to the Lord,
   And so shall thy plans succeed.
4 God created each thing for an end of its own,
   Yea, even the wicked for the day of disaster.
5 All the proud-minded the Lord abhorreth;
   Assuredly[3] none shall escape unpunished.
6 By kindness and faithfulness sin is atoned for,
   And through fear of the Lord men escape disaster.[4]
7 When the Lord is pleased with the ways of a man,
   He makes even his foes to become his friends.
8 Better a little, with righteousness,
   Than great revenues with injustice.
9 Man planneth out his way,
   But the Lord directeth his steps.

10 The lips of the king[5] are an oracle,
    And the sentence he utters infallible.
11 Balance and scales[6] are the Lord's,[7]
    All the weights of the bag[8] are His work.

Proverbs

12 Kings shrink with abhorrence from wrong-doing,
   For a throne is established by righteousness.
13 Honest lips are a king's delight ;
   He loveth the man that speaks truly.
14 The wrath of a king bodeth death,
   But a wise man knows how to appease it.
15 When the king's face shines, there is life :
   Like a cloud of spring-rain is his favour.

16 Wisdom is better to win than gold,
   And understanding is choicer than silver.
17 The path of the upright avoids misfortune ;
   He guardeth his life who gives heed to his way.[9]
18 Pride goeth before destruction,
   And a haughty spirit before a fall.[10]
19 Better be lowly of mind with the poor
   Than divide the spoil with the great.
20 He that gives heed to the word[11] shall be prosperous ;
   Happy the man that trusteth the Lord.
21 Wise men are called men of insight,
   And winsome speech adds to persuasiveness.
22 To a wise man is wisdom a fountain of life,
   But fools are chastised by their folly.
23 A wise mind uttereth thoughtful speech,
   And toucheth the lips to persuasiveness.
24 Winsome words are a honeycomb,
   Sweet to the soul and healing to the body.
25 Many a way seems straight to a man
   Which leads at the last to death.[12]
26 The labourer's appetite labours for him,
   For his (hungry) mouth urges him on.
27 A depraved man diggeth (a pit of) mischief,
   While his lips are touched as with scorching fire.

The Wisdom Books

28 A false man scattereth discord,
   And a whisperer separates friends.
29 A man of violence enticeth his neighbour,
   And leadeth him into a hurtful way.
30 He that closeth his eyes is devising some lie;
   He that tighteneth his lips hath concocted some mischief.
31 The grey head is a crown of glory,
   Which is won by a righteous life.
32 Patience is better than warrior's strength,
   And to rule o'er oneself than to capture a city.
33 The lot is cast into the lap,
   But the issue lies wholly with God.

xvii.
1 Better a bit of dry bread, with peace,
   Than a house full of feasting and strife.
2 A wise slave becomes lord of a profligate son;
   He will share the estate with the brothers.
3 Like the smelter for silver, the furnace for gold,[1]
   Is the Lord who testeth the heart.
4 A bad man gives heed to wicked words;
   A false man listens to mischievous speech.
5 He that mocketh the poor revileth his Maker;[2]
   He that joys at misfortune shall not go unpunished.
6 The crown of old men is children's children,
   And the glory of children is their father.
7 On the lips of a fool honest[3] words are unseemly;
   Much more lying words on the lips of a noble man.
8 A bribe is like a magic stone;[4]
   He that offers it prospers wherever he turns.
9 He that covers up wrong seeketh love,
   But the gossip estrangeth his friend.

Proverbs

10 A rebuke cuts[5] a wise man more deeply,
   Than a hundred stripes cut a fool.
11 The bad man is bent on playing the rebel;
   So a pitiless angel[6] is sent against him.
12 Meet a bear robbed of her whelps
   Rather than a fool in his folly.
13 Misfortune shall haunt the house
   Of the man who for good returns evil.
14 Strife may be started by idle words;[7]
   So give over contention before there is quarrelling.[8]
15 To acquit the guilty and condemn the innocent
   Are both alike to the Lord detestable.
16 Why does the fool bring a fee
   To buy wisdom, when he has no mind?
17 A (true) friend loveth at all times;
   A brother is born for adversity.
18 He that giveth his hand[9] is a fool—
   The man who goes bail for another.[10]
19 He loveth wounds[11] who loveth strife,
   And the man who builds loftily[12] seeketh destruction.
20 The false heart findeth no good,
   And the wily tongue comes to disaster.
21 A man begetteth a fool to his sorrow;
   No joy can there be for the father of a fool.
22 A happy heart is a healthful medicine,
   But a broken spirit dries up the bones.
23 The wicked accept a bribe[13]
   To deflect the course of justice.
24 The man of good sense has his gaze fixed on wisdom,
   But a fool has his eyes at the end of the earth.

The Wisdom Books

25 A foolish son is a grief to his father,
   And bitterness to her that bore him.
26 Since it is not right even to fine the innocent,
   To scourge men of honour is utterly wrong.[14]
27 He that spareth his words is truly wise,
   And a cool-tempered man is a man of discretion.
28 Even a fool may, if silent, be taken for wise—
   For a man of good sense, if he keeps his lips closed.

xviii.
1 The[1] estranged friend seeks an occasion[2] (of quarrel);
   He tries by all means to stir up strife.
2 A fool has no pleasure in prudence,
   But only in self-display.[3]
3 Wrongdoing brings down contempt,
   And disgrace follows dishonour.
4 The words that are found on (wise) lips are deep waters,
   A bubbling brook, a fountain of life.[4]
5 It is wrong to favour the guilty,
   To give verdict against the innocent.
6 A fool by his talk is involved in disputes,
   And his words cry aloud for a beating.
7 The mouth of a fool is his ruin;
   His lips are a snare to him.
8 Slanderous words are like dainty morsels;
   Down they glide to the innermost being.[5]
9 He that is slack in his business
   Is brother to him that destroys.[6]
10 The Lord[7] is a mighty tower;
   The righteous run in and are safe.
11 A rich man's wealth is his fortified city,[8]
   And like a high wall are his riches.[9]

Proverbs

12 Pride of heart goeth before destruction,[10]
   And before honour goeth humility.[11]
13 For a man to answer before he has heard
   Is folly and shame to him.
14 A man's spirit sustaineth his weakness,
   But a crushed spirit who can bear?
15 A sensible mind acquires knowledge,
   And a wise ear seeketh out wisdom.[12]
16 Presents prepare a man's way,
   And bring him before the great.
17 The first man to plead seems right,
   But then comes the other and tests him.
18 The lot puts an end to disputes,
   And decides between the mighty.
19 The rich man's wealth is his fortified city;
   His riches resemble the bars of a fortress.[13]
20 A man's words will bear for him plenty of fruit,
   And his speech shall have an abundant harvest.
21 Death and life are in the power of the tongue,
   And those who love[14] it must eat its fruit.
22 He that findeth a wife hath found a blessing,
   And won a sign of the Lord's good will.
23 A poor man speaks like a suppliant,
   But the rich man answereth gruffly.
24 There are friends that seek nothing but company,[15]
   And a friend that clings closer than brother.

xix.
1 Better[1] a poor man whose life is blameless
   Than one who is crooked,[2] although he be rich.[3]
2 To act without knowledge is foolish;[4]
   The hasty foot misses the goal.
3 A man ruins his life by his folly,
   And then he fumes against God.

The Wisdom Books

4 Wealth adds many friends,
   But the friend of the poor man withdraws.[5]
5 A false witness shall not go unpunished;
   He that uttereth lies shall not escape.[6]
6 To the liberal many pay court;
   All are friends of the man who gives.
7 A poor man's brothers all hate him;
   Much more do his friends stand aloof.[7]
8 He loveth his life that acquireth wisdom,[8]
   And he findeth good who observes understanding.
9 A false witness shall not go unpunished;
   He that uttereth lies shall perish.
10 A luxurious life for a fool is unseemly;
   Much more for a servant to rule over princes.
11 By forbearance a man shows his wisdom;
   To ignore an offence is his glory.
12 The wrath of a king is like the growl of a lion,[9]
   His favour like dew on the grass.
13 A silly son is his father's ruin,
   And a quarrelsome wife is an endless drip.[10]
14 House and wealth come to men from their fathers,
   But a prudent wife is the gift of the Lord.
15 Indolence ends in a deep heavy sleep,
   And the man that is slack shall be hungry.
16 He that keeps the commandment preserveth his life;
   He that spurneth the word[11] shall die.
17 To be kind to the poor is to lend to the Lord,
   Who will pay the good deed back.
18 Chastise thy son, while yet there is hope,
   And set not thy heart on having him ruined.[12]
19 He who payeth a fine is very angry,
   But, if he should scoff, he must pay still more.[13]

Proverbs

20 Listen to counsel, receive instruction,
   That thou mayest be wise in the days to come.[14]
21 A man has many a plan in his mind;
   But the Lord has His purpose—and that will stand.
22 A man's kindness brings him return;[15]
   Better be poor than a cheat.
23 The fear of the Lord is the pathway to life,
   To that quiet content which no evil can visit.
24 The lazy man buries his hand in the dish,
   And refuses to carry it back to his mouth.[16]
25 When a scoffer is beaten, a simpleton learns,
   But reproof is enough to teach sensible men.[17]
26 That son is a thorough disgrace and scoundrel
   Who maltreats his father and drives out his mother.
27 Cease, my son, to despise[18] instruction,
   To wander away from the words of knowledge.
28 An unprincipled witness scoffs at justice,
   And the mouth of the wicked pours out[19] wrong.
29 The scourge[20] is prepared for the scoffer,
   And stripes for the back of the fool.

XX.

1 Wine is a mocker, strong drink is a brawler,
   And whoso reels under it acteth not wisely.[1]
2 The wrath of a king is like the growl of a lion,[2]
   And he who provokes him endangers his life.
3 It honours a man to keep from strife,
   But every fool showeth his teeth.
4 In autumn the lazy man will not plough;
   So in harvest he asks for a crop in vain.
5 A plan may lie deep in the heart like (well-) water,
   But a skilful man knows how to draw it up.

The Wisdom Books

6 Many a man professes kindness,
   But a man of fidelity who can find?
7 Happy the sons that come after the man
   Whose life has been righteous and blameless.
8 Throned on the seat of judgment,
   The king sifts all wrong with his eyes.[3]
9 Who can say, " I have cleansed my heart,
   Pure and sinless am I " ?
10 Divers weights and divers measures
   Are both alike to the Lord detestable.[4]
11 Even a child is known by his deeds,
   As his conduct is good or bad.[5]
12 The hearing ear and the seeing eye
   Are both alike the Lord's creation.
13 Love not sleep, lest thou come to poverty;
   Open thine eyes, that thy bread may be plentiful.
14 " Bad, bad," says the buyer;
   But when he is gone, he brags.
15 Lips of wisdom are store of gold,
   Wealth of coral and precious vessels.
16 Take[6] the garment of him who goes bail for another,
   And hold it[7] in pledge for that other.
17 Bread won by deception tastes sweet to a man,
   But at last his mouth shall be filled with gravel.
18 Take advice in arranging thy plans,
   And do not make war without guidance.
19 Who carries tales divulges secrets;[8]
   Have nothing to do with a gossip.
20 He that curseth his father or mother—
   His lamp will go out in thick darkness.
21 Wealth hastily gotten at first
   Will remain unblessed in the end.

Proverbs

22 Do not say, " I will pay back evil";
  But wait for the help of the Lord.
23 Divers weights the Lord abhorreth;[9]
  False balances are not good.
24 Since the Lord controls a man's steps,
  How can man understand his way?
25 A man is ensnared if he dedicates rashly,[10]
  And only makes inquiry after his vow.
26 A wise king winnows the wicked,[11]
  And passes the wheel[12] over them.
27 The spirit of man is the lamp of the Lord,
  Searching every room of his being.
28 Kindness and faithfulness guard the king,
  And his throne is established by justice.[13]
29 The glory of youth is its strength,
  But grey hair is the beauty of age.
30 A bad man is doomed[14] to the lash, whose stripes
  Will cut to his inmost soul.

xxi.
1 The Lord guides the king's heart like watercourses,
  Turning it whither He will.
2 A man's life may seem thoroughly straight to himself,
  But the Lord weigheth the heart.[1]
3 The doing of justice and right
  To the Lord is more welcome than sacrifice.[2]
4 A haughty look, a heart of pride,
  The soil[3] of the wicked is sin.
5 The plans of the diligent issue in gain,
  But overmuch haste leadeth only to want.
6 He[4] that winneth him wealth by a fraudulent tongue
  Is pursuing a breath and a deadly snare.

The Wisdom Books

7 The violence of the wicked shall sweep them away,
   Because they refuse to act justly.
8 The way of the vicious[5] is crooked,
   But a pure man does what is straight.
9 It[6] is better to live on the roof[7] in a corner,
   Than in a spacious house with a quarrelsome woman.
10 The wicked man's passion is all to do harm;
   He looks on his neighbour with pitiless eye.
11 When a scoffer is punished, a fool becomes wise;
   But the wise are receptive, and learn by instruction.[8]
12 The Lord considers the righteous,
   But the house of the wicked He overthrows.[9]
13 He that stoppeth his ears at the cry of the poor
   Shall find his own call unanswered.
14 A gift in secret extinguisheth[10] anger,
   And a bribe in the bosom (soothes) strong indignation.
15 When justice is done, the righteous rejoice;
   But evil-doers are ruined.
16 The man who strays from wisdom's way
   Shall rest where the dead[11] are gathered.
17 The lover of pleasure will come to want,
   And lovers of wine and oil cannot grow rich.
18 For the righteous the wicked is ransom;
   The false take the place of the upright.[12]
19 It is better to dwell in a desert land
   Than with a provoking and quarrelsome woman.[13]
20 In the wise man's homestead is precious treasure,[14]
   But a silly man swallows it up.
21 The pursuit of justice and kindness
   Is crowned with life[15] and honour.

Proverbs

22 The wise man scales the strong men's city,
    And brings down the stronghold in which they trusted.
23 He that guardeth his mouth and his tongue
    Preserveth himself from trouble.
24 Scoffers men call the proud and haughty
    Who act with insolent pride.
25 The desire of the sluggard shall slay him,
    For his hands refuse to work.
26 Desires and petitions are endless,[16]
    But the righteous giveth unsparingly.
27 The sacrifice of the wicked is detestable;
    Much more when offered with vile intent.
28 A lying witness shall perish,[17]
    But a trustworthy witness shall stand for ever.[18]
29 The wicked put on a bold face,
    But the upright take heed to[19] their conduct.
30 No wisdom nor understanding
    Nor counsel can match[20] the Lord.
31 For the day of battle the horse may be harnessed,
    But only the Lord can dispense the victory.

xxii.
1 A fair name is more to be chosen than wealth;
    Men's regard is far better than silver and gold.
2 The rich and the poor meet together;
    The Lord is the Maker of both.[1]
3 The prudent scent mischief and hide;
    The simple go on and are punished.[2]
4 The reward of the humble who fear the Lord
    Is riches and honour and life.
5 On the way of the crooked lie traps[3] and snares;
    He who watches his life will keep far away.

6 Train up a child for his destined way,[4]
   And, even when old, he will not depart from it.
7 The rich lords it over the poor,
   And the borrower is slave to the lender.
8 He that sows wrong shall reap trouble,
   And the gain he has toiled for shall vanish.[5]
9 The man with the kindly eye shall be blessed,
   For he gives of his bread to the poor.
10 Expel the scoffer and discord will vanish,
   And strife and insult cease.
11 The pure in heart are beloved of the Lord,[6]
   And the winsome of speech have the king for a friend.[7]
12 The Lord is watching, alert and aware,[8]
   And the aims of the false He subverteth.
13 The lazy man saith, "There's a lion outside,
   On the street I am like to be murdered."[9]
14 The lewd woman's mouth is a deep, deep pit;[10]
   He who angers the Lord will fall into it.
15 Folly is bound to the mind of a child,
   But the rod of correction removes it.
16 He who crushes the poor in the end but enriches him,
   But a gift to the rich only tends to his poverty.[11]

SECOND COLLECTION OF PROVERBS[1]
(xxii. 17—xxiv. 22)

xxii.
17 Incline[2] thine ear and hear my words,[3]
   And set thy heart to know their beauty.
18 Keep them in thy mind,
   Have them ever fixed on thy lips.
19 That thy trust may be in the Lord
   I teach thee them this day,
20 As I wrote for thee heretofore
   Concerning counsels of wisdom—
21 To acquaint thee with words of truth,
   And with answers for those who would question[4] thee.

22 Rob not the poor because he is poor,
   And crush not the weak in the gate ;
23 For the Lord will defend their cause,
   And will rob of their lives those who rob them.

24 Make no friend of a man prone to anger,
   Nor go with a man of passion,
25 In case thou learn his ways,
   And get thyself ensnared.

26 Be not one of those that give pledges,[5]
   Of those that are surety for debt ;
27 For if thou hast nothing to pay,
   Thy bed[6] will be taken from under thee.

28 Remove not the ancient landmark,
   Established by thy fathers.

The Wisdom Books

29 Seest thou a man expert in his business ?
   He shall stand in the presence of kings,
   But before obscure men he shall not stand.

xxiii.
1 If thou sit at a ruler's table,
   Consider well who[1] is before thee ;
2 And set a knife to thy throat,
   If thou be a hearty eater.

4[2] Toil not to make thyself rich,
    Desist from this thy purpose ;
5   For no sooner seen[3] than gone.
    For riches make themselves wings,
    Like an eagle that flies towards heaven.

6 Do not dine with a niggardly man,
   And do not fancy his dainties ;
7   For a reckoning soul hath he.[4]
    He tells thee to eat and drink,
    But his heart is not with thine.
8*a* Thou must spit out the piece thou hast eaten,
3*b*   For it is bread of deceit.

9 Speak not in the ears of a fool,
   For thy wisest words he despises—
8*b*   Thy fair discourse is in vain.

10 Remove not the widow's[5] landmark,
    Nor enter the fields of the fatherless ;
11 For they have a mighty Champion,
    Who will plead their cause against thee.

12 Apply thy mind to instruction,
    Thine ear to the words of knowledge.

Proverbs

13 Leave not a child unchastised,
    For thy beating will save him from death.[6]
14 It is for thee to beat him,
    And so shalt thou save him from Sheol.
15 My son, if thy heart be wise,
    Then my heart too will be glad.
16 Yea, I shall rejoice from my soul,
    When thy lips utter words of rectitude.
17 Be not envious of sinners,
    But ever fear the Lord ;
18 For there is a future for thee,
    And thy hope shall not be cut off.

19 Listen, my son, and be wise,
    And walk in the way of prudence.[7]
20 Mix not with men that drink wine,
    Or that gorge themselves with flesh ;
21 For gorging and drink make men paupers,
    And drowsiness covers with rags.

22 Listen to the father that begat thee,
    And despise not thine aged mother ;[8]
25 But let thy father be glad,
    And make thy mother happy.
24 For a righteous son makes a glad, glad father,
    And a prudent son is the joy of his mother.

26 Give heed to me, my son,
    Let thine eyes take note of my ways.
27 For a deep, deep pit is the harlot,[9]
    The lewd[10] woman a narrow well.
28 Yea, she lies in wait like a robber,
    And many are they she plunders.

The Wisdom Books

The Peril of Wine

29 Who is it that cries, " Ah ! Woe is me ! "
    Who is it that hath quarrels and plaints ?
    Who is it that hath senseless bruises ?
    And who hath the dull red eyes ?
30 Those that linger over wine,
    Those that drink spiced wine with a relish.
31 Look not on the ruddy wine,
    When in the cup it sparkles.
    Smoothly it glideth down ;
32 But at last it bites like a serpent,
    And stingeth like an adder.
33 Strange things thine eyes behold,
    Thy mind and thy speech go a-wandering ;
34 Like one riding the sea[11] art thou
    In the throes of a violent storm.
35 " I[12] was struck, but I feel no pain.
    Of the blows I am all unconscious.
    O when shall I wake (from my wine) ?
    I would seek it once again."

xxiv.
1 Be not envious of evil men,
    And do not desire to be with them ;
2 For they cherish designs of plunder,
    And mischief is on their lips.

3 By wisdom a house is built up,
    By intelligence it is established ;
4 By knowledge its chambers are filled
    With all precious and pleasant substance.

5 Wise men are better than strong men,[1]
    And knowledge is better than might ;

Proverbs

6 For wars are waged by wise guidance,
And victory lieth in counsellors.

7 Wisdom is too high for a fool;
So he opens not his mouth in the gate.
8 The man who deviseth mischief
Is known among men as a schemer.
9 The scheming of fools is sin,
And the scoffer is hated of men.

10 If thou hast been slack, in the day of distress
Thy resource will be scanty.[2] .
11 Rescue those that are taken to death;
Save those that are tottering to slaughter.
12 If thou say, " It is not in my power,"[3]
He that weigheth the heart, *He* discerns ;
He that watcheth thy soul, *He* knows,
And on each He will bring back his deeds.

13 As the honey thou eatest, my son, is wholesome,
And sweet to thy taste is the honeycomb,
14 Even so, be assured, to thy soul is wisdom.[4]

15 Lie not in wait[5] for the home of the just,
And do not assail his dwelling-place ;
16 For the just, though he fall seven times, shall rise,
But the wicked shall stumble to ruin.

17 At the fall of thy foe rejoice not,
And do not exult at his overthrow ;
18 Lest the Lord be displeased when He sees it,
And turn His anger away from him.

19 Be not fretful because of evil-doers,
Nor envious of the wicked ;

20 For the bad man shall have no future,
   The lamp of the wicked is quenched.

21 Fear the Lord, my son, and the king,
   Be not haughty to one or the other ;[6]
22 For swift is the ruin they raise,
   The disaster they send unforeseen.

APPENDIX TO THE SECOND COLLECTION OF PROVERBS (xxiv. 23—34)

23   These also belong to the wise men :

   It is wrong to be partial in (giving of) judgment.[7]
24 All men shall curse and all people shall execrate
   Him that pronounceth the guilty man innocent.
25 But those whose decisions are just shall fare pleasantly;
   Blessings of fortune shall rest upon them.

26 As one who kisses the lips[8]
   Is he who returns a straight answer.

27 Set thy business in order without,
   Make all ready in thy fields :
   After that[9] thou mayest build up thy house.

28 Bear not false witness against thy neighbour,
   Nor let thy lips be deceitful.
29 Do not threaten to treat him as he treated thee,
   And to visit his deed with retribution.

On the Sluggard

30 By the field of the sluggard I passed,
   By the vineyard of one that was foolish.

Proverbs

31 And lo! it was all overgrown with thistles;
　　Its surface was covered with nettles;
　　Its wall of stone was in ruins.
32 As I looked, I thought upon it,
　　And I drew from the sight a lesson.
33 " Just³ a little more sleep, a little more slumber,
　　A little more lying with folded hands."
34 So shall poverty come upon thee like a robber,
　　And want like an armed man.

THIRD COLLECTION OF PROVERBS (xxv.—xxix.)

xxv.
1 These also are proverbs of Solomon, which the men of Hezekiah, king of Judah, copied out.

2 The glory of God is His mystery,
  But the glory of kings[1] is investigation.
3 Like the height of the heavens and the depth of the earth,
  So the purpose of kings is unsearchable.

4 Remove the dross from silver,
  And forth it comes pure altogether.[2]
5 Remove wicked men from the king,
  And his throne is established by righteousness.

6 In the presence of a king claim not honour,
  Nor stand in the place of the great.
7a Better be told, " Come up hither,"
7b Than be humbled before the prince.

8a Do not hastily bring up a law-suit
7c   Of something thine eyes have seen.
8b For what wilt thou do in the end,
8c   When thy neighbour hath put thee to shame ?
9 Discuss the affair with thy neighbour,
  Reveal not his secret to others ;
10 Lest those that have heard it reproach thee,
  And thine infamy pass not away.

11 (Like) apples[3] of gold in carvings of silver
  Is a word that is fittingly spoken.

Proverbs

12 (Like) an earring of gold and a necklace of fine gold
   Is a wise man's reproof to a listening ear.
13 Like a (drink) cooled by snow in the time of harvest
   Is a faithful envoy to those that send him :
   He refreshes the soul of his master.
14 As clouds and wind that yet bring no rain,
   So is one that boasteth of gifts that he gives not.
15 An angry man[4] can be won by forbearance,
   And bones can[5] be broken by gentle words.
16 If thou findest honey, eat just what thou needest,
   Lest, after a surfeit, thou vomit it up.
17 In the house of thy friend let thy foot be but seldom,
   Lest, sated with thee, he detest thee.
18 One that beareth false witness against his neighbour
   Is a hammer, a sword, and a sharp-pointed arrow.
19 In a crumbling tooth and a foot unsteady
   Is the faithless man's trust in the day of distress.
20 As[6] vinegar to a wound[7]
   Is a song to a sorrowful heart.
21 Give thine enemy food, if he hunger ;
   And water, if he be thirsty :
22 For so shall thou heap coals of fire on his head,
   And the Lord shall give thee recompense.
23 As the north wind bringeth forth rain,
   So slander an angry countenance.
24 It[8] is better to live on the roof in a corner
   Than in a spacious house with a quarrelsome woman.
25 Like cool water to one that is weary
   Is good news from a distant land.
26 Like a fountain befouled or a ruined spring
   Is a just man who falleth before the wicked.

The Wisdom Books

27 It is not good to eat much honey;
   Be sparing then of thy compliments.[9]
28 Like a city whose walls are broken down
   Is a man without self-control.

xxvi.
1 In a fool is honour as unbecoming
  As snow in summer or rain in harvest.
2 Like the (aimless) flight of a sparrow or swallow,
  The curse that is baseless does not come home.
3 A whip for the horse, a bridle for the ass,
  And a rod for the back of fools.[1]
4 Do not answer a fool as beseems his folly,
  In case thou, too, become like him.
5 Answer a fool as beseems his folly,
  Lest he fancy himself to be wise.
6 To send a fool with a message
  Is to cut off one's feet and to drink disaster.[2]
7 Like the limp[3] legs of the lame
  Is a proverb in the mouth of a fool.
8 Like a bundle of jewels on a heap of stones[4]
  Is honour conferred on a fool.
9 Like a thorn-stick brandished by a drunken man[5]
  Is a proverb in the mouth of a fool.
10 All fools must suffer sore anguish of body,
   And their insolence shall be shattered.[6]
11 Like a dog that returns to his vomit,
   A fool repeateth his folly.
12 If thou seest a man who thinks himself wise,
   There is far more hope for a fool than for him.[7]

On the Sluggard

13 The lazy man saith, " There's a lion on the road,
   There's a lion on the street."[8]

Proverbs

14 As the door turns on its hinges,
   So the lazy man in his bed.
15 The lazy man buries his hand in the dish—
   Too weary to carry it back to his mouth.[9]
16 The lazy man thinks himself wiser
   Than seven who can answer discreetly.

17 To mix in a quarrel not your own
   Is to catch a dog by the ears.
18 Like a madman who hurleth about
   Deadly fire-brands and arrows,
19 Is the man who deceiveth his neighbour
   And says that he did it in jest.
20 In the absence of wood the fire goes out,
   In the absence of slander contention ceases.
21 As charcoal to embers or wood to fire
   Is a quarrelsome man for kindling strife.
22 Slanderous words are like dainty morsels,
   Down they glide to the innermost being.[10]

On Hypocrisy

23 Like a sherd overlaid with silver slag
   Is a wicked heart with glowing [11] lips.
24 With his lips one who hates (thee) dissembles,
   But he cherishes guile in his heart.
25 When he speaketh thee fair, trust him not :
   In his heart lurk hateful things seven.
26 One who veileth his hatred with guile
   Has his malice uncovered in public.
27 He that diggeth a pit shall fall into it ;
   He that rolleth a stone gets it back upon him.
28 A false tongue bringeth destruction ; [12]
   A flattering mouth worketh ruin.

The Wisdom Books

xxvii.
1 Boast not thyself of to-morrow,
   For thou knowest not what a day may bring forth.
2 Let another mouth praise thee, not thine—
   The lips of some other, not thine.
3 A stone is heavy and sand is weighty,
   But heavier than both the vexation caused by fools.
4 Indignation is fierce, anger pours like a flood;
   But who can stand before jealousy?
5 Better an open reproof
   Than affection that is concealed.
6 The wounds of a friend are sincere,
   But profuse[1] are the kisses of a foe.
7 Honey is scorned by a man that is full,
   But anything bitter is sweet to the hungry.
8 Like a bird that strays from its nest
   Is a man that wanders from home.
9 Oil and perfume rejoice the heart,
   But sorrow of spirit doth rend it asunder.[2]
10 Thy friend and thy father's friend forsake not;
   And in thy day of distress
   Do not enter the house of thy brother.[3]
   Near neighbour is better than distant brother.
11 Be wise, my son, and gladden my heart,
   That so I may answer the man who would taunt me.
12 The prudent scent mischief and hide;
   The simple go on and are punished.[4]
13 Take the garment of him who goes bail for another,
   And hold it in pledge for that other.[5]
14 If early in the morning
   One loudly blesses another,
   It is reckoned to him as a curse.

Proverbs

15 An endless drip on a rainy day
 And a quarrelsome wife are alike ;[6]
16 He hideth the wind that would hide her,
 And his hand graspeth at oil.[7]
17 As iron sharpens iron,
 So a man sharpens his friend.
18 He that tendeth a fig-tree shall eat its fruit ;
 So one who attends to his lord will get honour.
19 As[8] face answers to face,
 So the mind of one man to another.[9]
20 Abaddon and Sheol [10] are ever unsated,
 And ever unsated the eyes of men.
21 As the smelter for silver, the furnace for gold,[11]
 So repute is the test of a man.
22 Though thou bray a fool with a pestle
 Along with bruised grain in a mortar,
 Thou wilt not get him rid of his folly.

Advice to Farmers

23 Look well to the state of thy flock,
 And give thy mind to thy herds ;
24 For wealth lasts not for ever,
 Nor riches[12] through all generations.
25 When the hay is removed and the new growth appears,
 And the grass of the uplands is (all) gathered in,
26 Then the lambs will supply thee with clothing,
 And the goats with the price of a field ;
27 And goats' milk enough there will be for thy food,[13]
 And a livelihood for thy maidens.

xxviii.
1 The wicked flee, when no man pursueth,
 But the righteous are bold as a lion.

The Wisdom Books

2   By the sin of the violent quarrels arise,
      But a man of sense will extinguish them.[1]
3   A wicked[2] man that oppresseth the poor
      Is a deluging rain that leaves no food.
4   Those who turn from instruction[3] admire the wicked,
      But those who observe it are zealous against them.
5   The wicked have no understanding of justice,
      But who cares for the Lord understands it completely.
6   Better a poor man whose life is blameless
      Than one who is crooked, although he be rich.[4]
7   A son that is prudent observeth instruction,[5]
      But the comrade of profligates shameth his father.
8   He that adds to his substance by interest or increase[6]
      But gathers for him that is kind to the poor.
9   If one turns a deaf ear to instruction,
      His very prayers are detestable.
10 He that turneth the upright to wicked ways
      Shall himself fall into the pit that he dug ;
      But the blameless shall come to prosperity.
11 A rich man may think himself wise,
      But a poor man with brains can see through him.
12 What a pageant there is, when the just are triumphant !
      When the wicked emerge into power, men hide.[7]
13 No man shall prosper that covers his sins,
      But those that confess and forsake them find mercy.
14 Happy the man that feareth[8] always,
      But the obstinate plunge to disaster.
15 A roaring lion, a prowling bear,
      Is a bad man who rules an impoverished people.

Proverbs

16 That prince has no prudence that plays the oppressor,
    But long shall he live that detests unjust gain.
17 He that sheddeth[9] the blood of a man—
    Let him flee to a city,[9] let none apprehend him.
18 The blameless life shall be kept in safety,
    But the crooked life shall suddenly[10] fall.
19 He that tilleth his land shall have plenty of bread,
    But idle pursuits end in plenty of poverty.[11]
20 A trustworthy man shall be richly blessed,
    But who hastes to get riches shall not go unpunished.
21 It is wrong for a man to be partial,[12]
    To sin for a piece of bread.
22 A greedy man[13] hastes to be rich,
    Not knowing that want shall befall him.
23 A man who reproves gets more thanks in the end
    Than a smooth-tongued flatterer.
24 One who robbeth his parents and says, "'Tis no sin,"
    Is companion to him that destroys.[14]
25 A greedy man stirreth up strife;
    He that trusts in the Lord shall flourish.[15]
26 He that trusts in himself is a fool;
    He that walketh in wisdom is safe.
27 He that gives to the poor shall not come to want,
    But who veileth his eyes shall have many a curse.
28 When the wicked emerge into power, men hide;[16]
    When they perish, the righteous increase.

xxix.
1 One who stiffens his neck against all reproof
    Shall be suddenly crushed beyond healing.
2 When the just are in power, the people are glad;
    When the wicked hold sway, the people groan.

The Wisdom Books

3 A man that loves wisdom brings joy to his father,
   But the comrade of harlots consumeth his substance.
4 By justice a king sets his country erect,
   But one whose exactions are heavy destroys it.
5 A man who cajoleth his neighbour
   Is spreading a net for his steps.
6 By his sin is a wicked man snared,
   But the righteous doth shout for joy.
7 To the righteous the cause of the poor is dear,
   But the wicked care nothing at all.
8 Scoffers inflame a city (with discord),
   But wise men turn passions aside.
9 When a wise man disputes with a fool,
   He[1] storms and laughs, and peace there is none.
10 Men of blood hate the blameless;
   The wicked[2] seek for his life.
11 The fool lets his temper go,
   But a wise man restraineth his anger.[3]
12 If a ruler pays heed to false tales,
   His officials all grow to be scoundrels.
13 Oppressor and poor meet together,
   But the light in the eyes of them both is the Lord's.[4]
14 If a king be faithful and just to the poor,
   His throne shall stand for ever.
15 The rod of correction brings wisdom,
   But a child let loose brings disgrace on his mother.
16 When the wicked hold sway, wrong increases,
   But the righteous shall gloat on their downfall.
17 Correct thy son and thy mind will be eased,
   And he will delight thy soul.

Proverbs

18 People break loose in the absence of vision,
    But he that observeth instruction is happy.
19 Not by words can a servant[5] be trained ;
    For he knows, but he will not obey.
20 Seest thou a man of hasty speech,
    There is far more hope for a fool than for him.[6]
21 The spoiled child will end as a servant,
    And come to grief at the last.[7]
22 A passionate man stirs up strife,
    And much evil is wrought by hot temper.
23 Pride will lay a man low,
    But the lowly attain unto honour.
24 His own foe is he who goes shares with a thief ;
    He heareth the curse, but he uttereth [8] nothing.
25 The fear of man bringeth a snare,
    But who trusteth the Lord is safe.
26 Many seek royal favour,
    But 'tis God decides every man's fate.
27 The righteous abhor the unjust,
    And the wicked abhor the upright.

COLLECTION OF BRIEF DISCOURSES AND APHORISMS (xxx. and xxxi.)

xxx.

1   The words of Agur, son of Jakeh, the Massaite.[1]
    Oracle of the man.

The Weary World-Problem

   I have wearied myself,[2] O God ;
     O God, I am weary and spent :
2 For dull as a brute am I,
     Not a man with the mind of a man.
3 I have not learned wisdom,
     And nothing I know of the Holy One.[3]
4 Who hath climbed the heavens and come down ?
     Who hath gathered the wind in his fist ?
   Who hath tied in a garment the waters,
     Or set up the bounds of the earth ?
   What is his name, or his son's name ?
     For surely thou knowest.[4]

5 The[5] words of God have all been tested,[6]
     He shieldeth those that take refuge in Him.
6 Unto His words add thou nothing at all,
     Lest He should convict thee of being a liar.

A Prayer for Preservation alike from Wealth and Poverty

7 For two things I entreat thee ;
     Deny me not, ere I die.
8 Put falseness and lying away from me ;
     Give me neither riches nor poverty,
     Grant me the food I need ;

Proverbs

9 Lest, if surfeited, I deny Thee,
  And say, " Who then is Jehovah ? "
  Or poverty drive me to steal,
  And profane the name of my God.

Against Defamation

10 To a master defame not his servant,
   Lest he curse thee and thou have to smart for it.

Four Evil Types

11 There are those that curse their fathers,
   And leave their mothers unblessed.
12 There are others that think themselves pure,
   Yet are all unwashed of their filthiness.
13 There are others with haughty eyes
   And supercilious eyebrows.
14 There are others whose teeth are swords—
   Yea, the teeth in their jaws are knives,
   To devour the poor from the earth,
   And the needy from off the ground.

Four Insatiable Things

15 There[7] are three things that never are satisfied—
   Four[8] that say never, " Enough ! "
16 Sheol;[9] the womb that is barren ;
   The earth unsated with water ;
   And fire that says never, " Enough ! "

Against Contempt ot Parents

17 The eye that mocketh a father,
   And scorneth an aged[10] mother,
   Shall be picked by the crows of the valley
   And clean devoured by vultures.

The Wisdom Books

Four Mysterious Things

18 Three things are too wonderful for me—
   Yea, four are beyond my knowledge:
19 The way of a vulture in air,
   The way of a snake on a rock,
   The way of a ship on the sea,
   And the way of a man with a woman.[11]

Four Intolerable Things

21 Under three things the earth doth tremble—
   Yea, four she cannot bear:
22 A slave when he comes to the throne,
   A fool who has more than enough,[12]
23 A plain [13] woman when she gets married,
   A maid that is heir to her mistress.

Four Things Little but Wise

24 Of the small things of earth there are four,
   And wiser they are than the wisest.[14]
25 The ants are a feeble folk,
   Yet they lay up their food in the summer.
26 A feeble folk, too, are the conies,
   Yet they make their house in the rocks.
27 The locusts again, though kingless,
   Yet march, every one, in good order.
28 And a lizard you could crush[15] in your hand
   Finds her way into royal palaces.

Four Stately Things

29 Three creatures there are whose step is stately,
   Yea, four whose step is majestic—
30 The lion, most valiant of beasts,
   Who in presence of foe never flinches;

Proverbs

31 The proud strutting[16] cock,[17] and the he-goat,
  And a king who is head of his army.[18]

32 Bluster thou not in arrogance,
  But lay thy hand on thy mouth.[19]

33 As the churning of milk yieldeth curd,
  And the wringing of the nose yieldeth blood,
  So the churning of wrath yieldeth strife.[20]

Against Immorality and Intemperance

xxxi.
1 The words of Lemuel, king of Massa,[1] which his mother taught him.

2 O son whom I bore, give heed to my words;
  And observe my sayings, thou son of my vows.[2]
3 Give not thy strength unto women,
  Nor thy love[3] unto those that slay kings.

4 Nor for kings is it right to drink wine,
  Or for princes to long for[4] strong drink;
5 Lest in drink they forget the law,
  And do wrong to the cause of the sorrowful.
6 But give drink unto him that is perishing,
  And wine to the bitter in soul;
7 That in drink he forget his poverty,
  And think of his sorrow no more.
8 Open thy mouth for the widow,[5]
  Do right by all fatherless children;[6]
9 Open thy mouth in just judgment,
  Defend the poor and the needy.

The Ideal Housewife

10 A woman[7] of worth who can find?
  Her price is far above corals.

11 To her her husband trusteth,
   And findeth no lack of gain.
12 She doeth him good and not harm
   All the days of his life.
13 She looketh out wool and flax,
   And worketh it up as she will.
14 Like the merchant-ships is she ;
   She bringeth her food from afar.
15 She riseth while yet it is night,
   And giveth her household food,
   And her maidens their portion appointed.
16 She examines a field and buys it ;
   With her earnings she planteth a vineyard.
17 She girdeth her loins with strength,
   And with vigour she plieth her arms.
18 She perceives that her profit is good ;
   Her lamp never goes out in the night.[8]
19 She layeth her hand on the distaff ;
   Her hand taketh hold of the spindle.
20 She stretcheth her hand to the poor,
   And her hand she extends to the needy.
21 She fears not the snow for her household ;
   Her household are all clad in scarlet.[9]
22 And coverlets she hath made her ;
   Her raiment is linen and purple.
23 In the gates is her husband well known,
   Where he sits with the elders in council.
24 Linen she makes and sells ;
   To the merchant she furnisheth girdles.
25 She is clothed with strength and glory ;
   She laughs at the days to come.
26 Her mouth she opens in wisdom ;
   Kind counsel is on her tongue.

Proverbs

27 She looks well to the ways of her household ;
    She eats not the bread of idleness.
28 Her children arise and bless her ;
    Her husband singeth her praises :
29 "Many daughters have done nobly,
    But thou excellest them all."
30 Grace is deceptive, and beauty is transient,
    But a woman of character[10]—*she* shall be praised.
31 Give her then what her hands have earned,
    Even the praise of her deeds in the gates.

ECCLESIASTES

ECCLESIASTES

i.
1   Discourses, by the Speaker[1], the son of David,[2] king in Jerusalem.

The Futility and Monotony of Nature and of Human Life

2 Utterest vanity ![3] The Speaker declareth :[4]
   Utterest vanity ![3] All is vanity.
3 What gain hath a man of all his toil
   Whereat he toileth under the sun?
4 The generations come and go,
   But evermore the earth abideth.
5 The sun doth rise, and the sun doth set,[5]
   But he panteth back to the place of his rising.
6 South the wind goeth, and northward it circleth;
   Circling and circling goeth the wind,
   And back on its circlings the wind returneth.
7 All the rivers run into the sea,
   But nevertheless is the sea not full.
   To the place to which the rivers run,
   Thither they run and run for ever.
8 All things are full of weariness,
   Of weariness unutterable.
   With all that it sees hath the eye no rest,
   And with all that it hears is the ear unfilled.

The Futility of the Search after Knowledge

9   What has been, shall be; what has happened already, will happen again: there is not a novelty
10 under the sun. When anything occurs that one is disposed to call really new, it will be found to have
11 happened already—ages before us. Nobody

remembers (to-day) the people of the olden time, and similarly the people of the after-time will not be remembered by anybody who comes after them.

12 I, the Speaker, was king over Israel in Jerusalem ;
13 and I gave my mind to the philosophic study and investigation of all that goes on under the sun. But a sorry business it is that God has given men to
14 busy themselves with. From my observation of all that goes on under the sun, I have come to the conclusion that it is all nothing but an illusion and a chasing of the wind.
15 That which is crooked can never be straightened,
And that which is lacking can never be counted.
16 Then I said to myself, Let me take my own case. I have amassed wisdom beyond all my predecessors in Jerusalem, and my experience of wisdom and of
17 knowledge has been a wide one ; but after applying my mind to the study of wisdom and knowledge, madness and folly, I am convinced that this also is a chasing of the wind ; for
18 Who is rich in wisdom is rich in vexation,
And increase of knowledge brings increase of pain.

The Futility of the Search after Pleasure

ii.
1 I said to myself, Well now, I will experiment with pleasure and indulge myself ; but I discovered with
2 surprise that this, too, was an illusion. I concluded that laughter was madness and joy a sterile thing.
3 I turned over in my mind how to cheer my senses with wine—preserving at the same time, however, my habitual wisdom¹—and how to embrace folly, until I should discover what satisfaction may be

Ecclesiastes

procured by men under heaven during the days
4 of their brief lives. I went in for enterprises on an
impressive scale. I had houses built and vineyards
5 planted. I had gardens laid out and parks planted
6 with all sorts of fruit trees. I had reservoirs constructed to water the trees that formed the plan-
7 tations. I bought male and female slaves in addition
to the others that had been born in my house. I had
cattle and sheep in abundance—far beyond my
8 predecessors in Jerusalem. Further, I amassed
silver and gold and treasure from (tributary) kings
and from the provinces. I procured male and female
singers and sensuous delights—concubines in
9 abundance; and richer and richer I grew beyond
all my predecessors in Jerusalem—taking care, how-
10 ever, to retain my wisdom. I refused my eyes
nothing that they longed for, and I did not abstain
from pleasure of any kind, for there was a pleasure
attached to all my effort, and the reward of all my
11 effort I found in that. But when I looked at all
the things my hands had made, and at the effort
that I had spent upon them, it all turned out to be
nothing but an illusion and a chasing of the wind:
12b here was no profit under the sun. For what will
the king's successor do but just what has been done
before?[2]

The Futility of Wisdom

12a   Then I turned to the consideration of wisdom and
13 madness and folly, and I saw that wisdom is as
superior to folly as light to darkness; for
14 While the wise have their eyes in their head,
The fool walketh in darkness.

The Wisdom Books

15 Still, I am well aware that in their fate they are both alike. So I said to myself, The fate of the fool shall be my fate also ; and what, in that case, am I the better for my pre-eminent wisdom ? So I
16 said to myself, Here is another illusion. For through all time the wise man is not remembered any more than the fool, seeing that in the days to come every one will be soon forgotten. Alas! the wise man
17 dies just like the fool. So life became odious to me, because I was vexed with all that goes on under the sun ; for it is all an illusion and a chasing of the wind.

The Futility of Work

18 Yes, all the effort that I had spent under the sun became odious to me, because I should have to
19 leave it to my successor ; and who can tell whether it will be a wise man or a fool that will have the disposal of the results of all my wise and earnest toil under the sun ? Here is another illusion.
20 Then I felt like yielding to despair because
21 of all my laborious toil under the sun ; for it may happen that a man who has toiled with wisdom, knowledge, and skill has to bequeath the results of it to another who has done no work upon it at all. Here, in this great evil, is another illusion.
22 For what does a man get from all the striving
23 and the strain of his work under the sun ? His days are all a torture, and his business a vexation : why, even the night brings no rest to his mind. Here is
24 another illusion. There is, then, no satisfaction for a man beyond eating and drinking and enjoying

Ecclesiastes

himself as he works. This I saw to be from God's
own hand ; for how can there be eating or enjoyment apart from Him ?[3]

26 For to the man who pleases Him He gives wisdom, knowledge and happiness ; to the sinner, on the other hand, He gives the task of gathering and amassing, that it may be given (in the end) to the man who pleases God.[1]

Here is another illusion and a chasing of the wind.

The Futility of Human Effort in the Light of the Fixed Order of the World

iii.
1 Everything has its season appointed,
   And every affair under heaven has its time.
2 A time to be born,
   And a time to die.
   A time to plant,
   And a time to uproot.
3 A time to slay,
   And a time to heal.
   A time to tear down,
   And a time to build up.
4 A time to weep,
   And a time to laugh.
   A time to mourn,
   And a time to dance.
5 A time to scatter stones,[1]
   And a time to clear them away.[2]
   A time to embrace,
   And a time to refrain.
6 A time to seek,
   And a time to lose.
   A time to preserve,
   And a time to throw away.

The Wisdom Books

7 A time to tear,
   And a time to sew.
   A time to be silent,
   And a time to speak.
8 A time to love,
   And a time to hate.
   A time for war,
   And a time for peace.
9 What does the worker gain by all his toil (thought
10 I) as I looked at the tasks that God has assigned to men to busy themselves with?

11 It is a beautiful[3] order that He has established—everything at its appointed time. Besides, He has planted in the human heart (the instinct for) eternity;[4] only men cannot discern the whole range—from beginning to end—of the work which God is carrying on.

12 I am convinced that the only satisfaction that can be theirs is to be happy and prosperous,[5] while
13 they live. Besides, it is God's own gift, when a man is privileged to eat, drink, and experience happiness in all his work.

14 I am convinced that all that God does is eternal; it is capable neither of increase nor of diminution:

and God has ordained this, in order to inspire men with reverence.[6]

15 Whatever is, has happened already; and what is yet to happen, already is: for that which has drifted[7] (into the past) God seeketh out again.

The Futility of Hoping for the Redress of Injustice in Some Future World

16 Once more, in the course of my observations under the sun, I saw that, in the place where judgments

were delivered, there was injustice—yes, injustice in the very place where justice should have been administered.

17 I said to myself, Yes, but *God* will judge the just and the unjust: for He hath appointed⁸ a time for every matter and for every act.⁹

18 I said to myself, It is for men's sake, that God may show them in their true light, and lead them
19 to see that they are but beasts. For the fate of men is the fate of beasts : their fate is one and the same. The one dies like the other. One breath is in them all, and man is no way superior to the
20 beasts. For all is but an illusion. All are on their way to the same place. All sprang from the dust,
21 and to the dust they shall all return. Who can tell whether¹⁰ the human spirit goes upward and the
22 spirit of the beast downward to the earth? So I recognised that there is no greater satisfaction for a man than to be happy in his work—that is his reward ; for, as to what is to happen after him— who can give him a glimpse of that ?

Man's Inhumanity to Man

iv.
1 Once more, I considered all the oppression that goes on under the sun. I saw the tears of the oppressed, who have no one to comfort them— power brutally wielded by the oppressors, and not
2 a soul to comfort them. Happy, thought I, were the dead who are already dead rather than the
3 living who are still alive ; but happier than either the creature that has never been born, to look upon the evil work that goes on under the sun.

The Wisdom Books

The Taint of Jealousy

4 Then I observed that all the laborious and skilful work of men has its origin and issue[1] in their jealousy of one another. Here is another illusion and a chasing of the wind.

The Wisdom of Unambitious Quiet

5 The fool foldeth his hands,
And his own flesh he devoureth.[2]
6 Better a single handful of quiet,
Than two handfuls of toil
And a chasing of the wind.

The Futility and Misery of Loneliness

7 Here is another of the illusions that I have
8 observed under the sun. Take, for example, a lonely man, with no one by his side—he has neither son nor brother: yet he toils on endlessly; his eye can never see money enough. "And yet, whom am I toiling for, and beggaring myself of happiness?" Here is another illusion, a sorry business indeed.

9 Two are better than one, for their toil is happily
10 rewarded. If, for example, one should fall, his comrade helps him to his feet: but woe betide the
11 man who falls, with nobody to help him up. Again, if two lie together, they get warm: but how can a man
12 get warm by himself? Again, while a solitary man may be overpowered, two can stand up to an assailant; while a cord that has three strands is not lightly snapped.

Ecclesiastes

The Futility of Wisdom—An Illustration

13 A young man that is poor but wise is better than a foolish old king who can no longer take a warning.
14 There was one such who passed from prison to the throne, though in the (old king's) reign he had been
15 born poor; and I observed that every man alive that walked under the sun supported his youthful
16 successor. Endless were the people who looked up to him as leader; and yet in later years their enthusiasm for him had vanished. Here is another illusion and a chasing of the wind.

Warnings against Insincerity and Rashness in the Discharge of Religious Duties

v.
1 Walk warily, when you go to the house of God: to participate in the worship with attentive ear[1] is better than the sacrifices offered by fools, who are only versed in the practice of wickedness.
2 Do not be rash with your tongue, and do not let your feelings hurry you into speech before God: for God is in heaven, while you are on earth; your words ought therefore to be few. For
3 As dreams proceed from multiplied cares,
   So the din of fools[2] from multiplied words.
4 When you make a vow to God, pay it without delay; for fools incur His displeasure. Pay
5 therefore what you vow. Better not vow than vow
6 and not pay. Do not allow your tongue to involve you in guilt and punishment;[3] and do not have to explain to the official[4] that it was a case of inadvertence (on your part). Why should you say things that must provoke God to bring your enterprises

7 to ruin ? for multiplied dreams and words bring multiplied vanities.[5] But hold God in reverence.

The Prevalence of Oppression

8 Do not be astonished when you see a poor man crushed, or right and justice plundered in a province ; for high officials are perpetually spying upon one another, and over them are others[6] higher still.

9 It is in every way an advantage to a land to have a king devoted to the cultivation of the soil.[7]

The Futility of Wealth

10 Who loves money can never have money enough,
   And the lover of riches no increase can satisfy.
   Here is another illusion.
11 Increase of wealth bringeth increase in those that consume it :
   What gain hath its owner save gazing on it with his eyes ?
12 Sweet is the sleep of the toiler, whether he eat much or little ; but the satiety of the wealthy man will not let him sleep.
13 One of the grievous evils that I have observed under the sun is this—wealth hoarded up to its
14 owner's ruin. The wealth vanishes in some sorry adventure ; and so, after becoming a father, he
15 finds himself with nothing at all.[8] Naked as he came from his mother's womb must he go again, just as he came. For all his toil he can take nothing away with him that he can carry in his
16 hand. This also is a grievous evil, that he must go away just as he came ; and what has he gained

Ecclesiastes

17 by toiling for the wind? Yes, all his days are spent in darkness and mourning,⁹ in deep vexation, sickness and anger.

18 I claim, as the result of my observation, that it is an excellent and comely thing (for a man) to eat, drink, and enjoy himself amid all his laborious toil under the sun during the days of the brief life

19 which God gives him: for that is his lot. Yes, when God gives a man wealth and riches and power to enjoy them, to take his share and be happy in

20 his work—this is a gift of God. Such a man will not think much about the brevity of his life; for his heart is touched by God to a glad response.[10]

The Futility of Wealth without the Power to Enjoy

vi.
1 One of the vexatious things that I have seen under
2 the sun to press heavily upon men is this. Take the case of a man to whom God has given wealth, riches, honour, everything heart can desire except the opportunity to enjoy it—that opportunity falling to some stranger. Here is a grievous and painful illusion.

3 If a man be the father of a hundred sons, and live for many long years, but without having enjoyed any true satisfaction from his prosperity and without the honour of burial (in the end), then such a man, I maintain, is not so fortunate as an untimely

4 birth, which, coming as a futility, departs in dark-
5 ness with its name enveloped in darkness, never having had sight or knowledge of the sunlight. It is this, rather than the other, that enjoys rest.

6 Though the man should live a thousand years twice

The Wisdom Books

over, yet enjoy no experience of happiness, are not both on their way to the same place?[1]

7 The toil of man is all for his mouth,
　Yet the appetite is unfilled.
8 What gain hath the wise man more than the fool,
　Or the poor man who walks through the world with discretion?
9 Better a glimpse with the eyes
　Than the roaming of the appetite.
　Here is another illusion and a chasing of the wind.

The Futility of the Struggle with Destiny

10 The character of what is has already been determined, and the destiny of man is already foreordained:[2] he cannot contend with one mightier
11 than himself. For multiplied words[3] mean but multiplied vanities; and what is man the better?
12 Who can tell what is good for man during his lifetime all the days of the brief and empty life that he passes like a shadow? Who can declare to a man what is to happen after him under the sun?

vii. Counsels for Conduct

1 A fair name is better than precious ointment,[1]
　And the day of death than the day of one's birth.
2 It is better to go to the house of mourning
　Than to go to the banqueting-house;
　Inasmuch as that[2] is the end of all men,
　And the living should lay it to heart.
3 Vexation is better than laughter;
　For, when the face is sad, it is well with the heart.[3]
4 The heart of the wise is in the house of mourning,
　But the heart of the fool in the house of mirth.

Ecclesiastes

5 It is better to hear the rebuke of the wise
   Than to lend one's ears to the song of a fool.
6 For like crackling of nettles under kettles,
   Even so is the cackle of fools.[4]
   Here is another illusion.
7 Extortion maketh the wise man mad,[5]
   And a bribe destroyeth the character.[6]
8 The end of a thing is better than the beginning,
   And patience is better than pride.
9 Do not be hastily vexed in thy temper;
   Vexation doth lodge in the bosom of fools.
10 Say not, " Why were the former days better than these ? "
   For such a question is not of wisdom.
11 As good as an inheritance is wisdom,[7]
   And gainful to those who behold the sun.
12 Wisdom defends, even as money defends;
   But herein is the greater gain of knowledge,
   That wisdom is life unto those that possess her.
13 Consider well the work of God;
   For who can make straight that which He hath made crooked?
14 In happy days be happy, and in the day of misfortune consider : for God has balanced the one against the other, in order to prevent men from discovering anything of the future.[8]

The Folly of Extremes

15 In the course of my illusory[9] life I have witnessed all sorts of things—honest men ruined by their very honesty, and unprincipled men who owe their
16 long life to their very lack of principle. Do not be over-pious or over-wise : why court destruction?

The Wisdom Books

17 But neither be over-wicked, nor play the fool:
18 why die before your time? It is good, while clinging to the one,[10] not to relax your grasp of the other;[11] for true religion avoids the excesses of both.[12]
19 Wisdom is a mightier protector to the wise than
20 ten men[13] who are in authority over a city. For[14] there is not a single righteous man upon earth— a man who does nothing but good and never falls into sin.
21 Further, pay no attention to current gossip, in case you may hear that your servant has cursed
22 you; for your conscience tells you that you too have cursed others many a time.

Woman a Delusion and a Snare

23 I subjected all this to the test of wisdom. I resolved to acquire wisdom, but she remained remote.
24 Yes, the essence of things remained remote—deep down in depths unfathomable.
25 Then, casting about, I gave my mind to the understanding and investigation of wisdom, to search after her for results, and to study the folly
26 of wickedness and the madness of folly. And a thing that I find to be more bitter than death is woman: for she is a veritable net, with her heart of snares and her hands of fetters. The man who enjoys the favour of God escapes her, but the sinner
27 is caught by her. Now mark this, says the Speaker. Putting one thing with another in order to arrive
28 at a conclusion—which, however, I have long and earnestly sought in vain—this at least I have discovered: that there is one man in a thousand—

Ecclesiastes

29 that I have discovered—but never a woman in all that number have I found. This only have I found—mark it well: that men were created upright by God, but they have sought out many contrivances of their own.

Reflections upon Despotism
viii.
1 Who is like the wise man?
Who is skilled in interpretation?
A man's wisdom illumines his face,
And a face that is harsh is transfigured.
2 Obey the king's commands; but, remembering
3 your oath to God, do not be drawn into hasty action. Leave his presence,[1] and do not embark upon any hurtful course[2]; for a king can do any-
4 thing he pleases, seeing that his royal word is authoritative, and his conduct unchallengeable.
5 He who keeps the commandment[3] will never come to harm.[4] The wise man knows in his heart
6 that there is an hour of judgment; for everything has its hour of judgment[5]—and men will be crushed
7 beneath the weight of calamity.[6] For they are ignorant of the future: who can tell what form it
8 will take? No man can control the day of his death, any more than he can control or restrain the wind. In war there is no discharge. Wrong will secure no immunity for the wrong-doer.
9 All this I saw, as I applied my mind to all that goes on under the sun, at a time when men were wielding their power over other men to ruin them.

The Wisdom Books

The Futility of Looking for a Moral Order in this World, and there is No Other

10 Thereafter I saw wicked men borne to the tomb from the holy place[7]—men who used to go about amid plaudits in the very city where they had so behaved.[8] Here is another illusion.

11f. Because[9] sentence is not swiftly executed upon deeds of wickedness, but a sinner may enjoy a long life though he do evil a hundred times over, men's hearts swell with the impulse to do evil; though sure I am that it will be well with those who fear God—I mean those
13 who really reverence Him—but it will not be well with the wicked: his life will be short as a shadow,[10] because he has no reverence for God.

14 Here is another of the anomalies[11] to be found upon the earth—honest men who fare as if they had been scoundrels, and scoundrels who fare as if they had been honest men. Here, methought, is another
15 futility. Then I commended mirth—for the only human satisfaction under the sun is to eat, drink, and be merry: these are the things that should accompany men during the days of the laborious life which God has given them under the sun.
16 When I gave my mind to the study of wisdom and to the observation of the business that is transacted in the world—for day and night one never
17 gets a glimpse of sleep[12]—then I recognised that man is impotent to discover the meaning of all the work of God that goes on under the sun. However laboriously men search, they will never discover it. A wise man may imagine he is on the point of
ix. understanding it, but he can never find it out.
1 For all this I laid to heart, and my heart[1] observed it all, that the just, the wise, and their doings are

Ecclesiastes

in the hand of God : no man knows whether it is to be love or hatred.[2] All that lies ahead of them is
2 vapour,[3] inasmuch as the fate of all is alike—of saint and scoundrel, good and bad,[4] pure and impure, those who do and those who do not practise sacrifice. Good man and sinner fare alike, those who take oaths and those who are afraid to take them.[5]
3 This is one of the vexing things that go on universally under the sun, that the fate of all is alike. Besides, the human heart is full of evil : all their life long, madness is in men's heart, and thereafter
4 they join the dead—not a man is left.[6] There is hope for all who are in life—a live dog even[7] is
5 better than a dead lion—for the living know at least that they have to die,[8] but the dead have no knowledge at all, and no further reward is possible
6 for them—their very memory is forgotten. Their love, hatred, jealousy, all alike have already vanished, and for all time they have no share in anything that goes on under the sun.

The Wisdom of Enjoyment

7 Go and eat thy bread with joy,
  And drink thy wine with a merry heart ;
  For what thou doest is God's good pleasure.[9]
8 At all times let thy raiment be white,[10]
  And let not oil on thy head be lacking.
9 Enjoy thy life with the woman thou lovest,
  All the days of thy fleeting life,
  Which He[11] hath given thee under the sun.
  For that is thy reward in thy life of laborious toil under the sun.
10 Do with thy might whatever thou hast in thy

The Wisdom Books

power to do ; for nothing can be done or devised, known or apprehended, in the under-world to which thou art going.

The Element of Chance in Life

11 Once more : I observed that under the sun it is not the swift that win the race, nor the strong that conquer in battle, neither is wisdom rewarded with bread, nor insight with wealth, nor intellect with practical appreciation ; all alike are the victims of
12 time and chance. Nobody knows his hour. Men are like fish caught in a net, or birds in a trap. Like them men are caught in the meshes in an evil hour, when suddenly it falls upon them.

The Place of Wisdom in Popular Esteem

13 The following illustration of wisdom came under
14 my notice, and it greatly impressed me. There was a small and thinly garrisoned town, which a powerful king came and invested by building huge
15 siege-works against it. But there happened to be in it a man, poor indeed, but endowed with a wisdom which enabled him to save the town. Not a soul,
16 however, remembered this poor man. So, me-thought, wisdom is better than strength ; yet the wisdom of a poor man is held in contempt, and his words are not listened to.[12]
17 Better wise words that are heard in quiet
    Than the shrieking of one who is lord among fools.
18 Better is wisdom than weapons of war,
    For one single blunder[13] may ruin much good.

Ecclesiastes

A Topsy-Turvy World
x.
5 Under the sun this evil I have seen,
    As 'twere the blundering order of a Ruler :[1]
6 The fool is set upon a lofty height,
    While men of wealth must take a lowly seat.
7 Slaves have I seen upon horse-back,
    And princes walking like slaves on the ground.

A Collection of Proverbs

1 As a deadly fly causes stench in the perfumer's ointment,
    So a little folly can ruin the rarest wisdom.
2 The sense of a wise man leads him to the right,[2]
    But the sense of a fool to the left.
3 As he goes on his way, a fool showeth his lack of sense ;
    And every one saith of him,[3] " There goes a fool."
4 If a ruler flare up in a passion against thee,
    Quit not thy post : for composure
    Can lull mighty passions[4] to rest.
8 He that diggeth a pit may fall therein,
    And a serpent may bite him that breaks through a wall.
9 He that quarrieth stones may be hurt by them,
    And the man who cleaves wood is imperilled thereby.
10 If the iron be blunt, and you whet not its edge,
    You must use more strength.
    He succeeds who can claim the advantage of wisdom.

The Wisdom Books

11 If a serpent bite for lack of enchantment,
   Then the skilful charmer hath no advantage.
12 The words of a wise man's mouth win him favour,
   But a fool by his lips is brought to ruin;
13 From the first the words of his mouth are folly,
   And the end of his speech is calamitous madness.
14 The fool maketh many words.
   Man knoweth not the future;
   And what shall happen after him,
   Who can declare unto him?
15 The fuss of fools must weary the man
   Who does not know his way to the town.[5]
16 Alas for thee, land! when thy king is a youth,
   And thy princes feast in the early morning;
17 But hail to thee, land! when thy king is a noble,
   And thy princes feast at the proper season,
   Like men and not like sots.
18 Through idleness the roof sinks in,
   And through slackness of hands does the house fall a-leaking.
19 Feasts are made for mirth,
   And wine cheers the heart of the living,
   And money answereth all things.
20 Even in thy thought[6] curse not the king,
   And curse not the rich in thy sleeping-chamber;
   For a bird of the air may carry the sound,
   And the thing that hath wings may declare the matter.

xi.
1 Cast thy bread on the face of the waters,
   For after many days thou shalt find it.
2 Give a portion to seven, yea, even to eight,[1]
   For thou knowest not what evil may come on the land.

Ecclesiastes

3 When the clouds are filled with rain,
   They empty it over the earth.
   If a tree[2] falls northward or southward,
   In the place where it falls it remains.
4 He who always is watching the wind
   Never gets to his sowing.
   He who always is scanning the clouds
   Never gets to his reaping.
5 As thou knowest not what is the way of the wind,
   Nor how the child[3] grows in the womb of the mother,
   So knowest thou not how God doth work—
   He who worketh in all things evermore.
6 In the morning sow thy seed,
   And till evening rest not thy hand;
   For thou knowest not which of the two shall prosper,
   Or whether both shall be good alike.

Rejoice, Young Man, in thy Youth : for the Sorrows of Age are Many and Sure

7 Sweet is the light, and pleasant it is
   For the eyes to behold the sun.
8 For, though a man live many years,
   All of them filled with gladness,
   Yet let him remember the days of darkness,
   For many shall they be.
   All that cometh is vapour.
9 Rejoice, young man, in thy youth,
   And keep thy young heart merry;
   Walk in the ways of thy heart,
   And in all that allureth thine eyes.
   But know that for all these things
   God will bring thee to judgment.[4]

The Wisdom Books

10 Put vexation away from thy mind,
    And banish all gloom[5] from thy body—
    For youth and life's dawn[6] are illusions—

xii.
1   But keep thy Creator in mind[1]
        In the days of thy prime :[2]

    Ere the gloomy days come on,
    And the years arrive when thou sayest,
    " No pleasure are they to me : "
2 The days when the sun grows dark,[3]
    And the light, and the moon, and the stars,
    And the rain is followed by clouds,
3 And the guards of the house[4] fall a-trembling,
    The mighty men[5] are bent,
    The grinders[6] cease, being few,
    Those that look through the windows[7] are darkened,
4 The doors[8] in the street are shut,
    When the sound of the mill[9] is low,
    And the twitter of birds is faint,[10]
    And the daughters of song are all feeble ;[11]
5 Yea, (the old) are afraid of a height,
    And the road is for them full of terrors,
    The almond-tree wears its blossoms,[12]
    The grasshopper limps along,[13]
    And the caperberry is powerless ;[14]
    For the man goes his way to his long, long home,
    And the mourners wander about the streets—
6 On the day when the silver cord is snapped,
    And the bowl (with the) golden (oil) is broken,
    And the pitcher is shattered over the spring,
    And the wheel falls into the cistern broken,

Ecclesiastes

7 And the dust goes back to the earth as it was,
   And the breath returns to the God who gave it.
8 Utterest vanity! The Speaker declareth:
   All is vanity.

A Later Addition in Praise of the Book, and, in general, of Wisdom

9 The Speaker, besides being wise, further instructed the people in knowledge, weighing and searching it out, and arranging it in the form of copious proverbs.
10 The Speaker made it his study to devise sayings that were at once true and attractive, and to record them in proper form.
11 The words of wise men, as collected,[15] are like goads, or like nails driven home; but they are (all) the gift of one shepherd.[16]
12 Beyond these, too, my son, take warning.
   Books are so many, their making is endless;
   And study protracted but wearies the flesh.

13 Hear the conclusion of the whole discourse:
   Reverence God and keep His commandments;
   For this is the essence of all that is human.
14 For God will bring every work to the judgment
   That is passed on all secret things, good or bad.

LAMENTATIONS

LAMENTATIONS

Lament over the Sorrows of Jerusalem[1]

Her Comfortless Doom

i.
1. Alas ! How lonely the city[2]
   Once crowded with people.
   She that was great among nations
   Is now as a widow.
   She that was queen of the provinces
   Now is a vassal.

2. Sore, sore she weeps in the night ;
   There are tears on her cheeks.
   Now there is no one to comfort
   Of all those that loved her.
   All of her friends have proved faithless,
   And turned to be foes.

3. From sorrow and toil into exile
   Hath Judah departed ;
   And now is her home with the heathen,
   And no rest she findeth.
   In the midst of her straits her pursuers
   Have all overtaken her.

4. The highways to Zion lie mourning,
   For pilgrims are none.
   All desolate now are her gates,
   And her priests are in sorrow.
   Her virgins are dragged away[3] far ;
   She herself is in bitterness.

Lamentations

5 Supreme her foes are now,
    And her enemies triumph.
  The Lord hath afflicted her sore
    For her manifold sins.
  Gone are her little ones captive
    In front of the foe.

6 The glory is vanished clean
    From the daughter of Zion.
  Her princes are like unto harts
    That can nowhere find pasture ;
  All feeble they move on their way
    With pursuers behind them.

7 Jerusalem calleth to mind
    The days of her travail,[4]
  When into the hands of the foemen
    Her people fell helpless.
  The mocking foe feasted his eyes
    On her sore desolation.

8 Jerusalem hath grievously sinned,
    And so she hath fallen.
  All they that honoured despise her
    At sight of her nakedness.
  She meanwhile groaneth and moaneth
    And turneth her backward.

9 Her filthiness clung to her skirts ;
    She became all abhorrent.
  To the future she gave not a thought,
    So her fall was appalling.[5]
  Behold, O Lord, what I suffer
    From the insolent foe.

Lamentations

10 The foeman hath stretched out his hand
    To secure all her treasures.
  The heathen she saw enter in
    And her temple profane—[6]
  Even those Thou forbadest to mix
    With Thine own congregation.

11 Her people all groan and moan
    In their search after bread.
  They have given away their treasures
    For food to revive them.
  Behold, O Jehovah, and see
    How abject am I.

12 All ye that pass by,[7] I appeal to you,
    Look ye and see;
  Has there ever been sorrow like mine,
    Like that dealt out to me,
  When the Lord, in His fierce indignation,
    Did put me to grief?

13 He hurled down fire from on high;
    It hath entered my bones.
  A net He hath spread for my feet;
    He hath turned me backward.
  Faint He hath left me and desolate
    All the day long.

14 A watch He hath kept on my sins;
    And into a yoke
  For my neck with His hands He hath twined them.
    Then, crippling my strength,
  He hath given me into the hands
    Of a foe irresistible.

Lamentations

15 The Lord hath hurled to the ground
   All the strong men within me.
   He hath summoned a festal assembly[8]
   To crush my young (warriors).
   The Lord in His wine-press hath trodden
   The daughter of Judah.

16 For these things I weep without ceasing;
   Mine eyes stream with tears;
   For none have I now by my side
   To refresh me and comfort me.
   My children are clean distraught,
   For the foe hath prevailed.

17 Zion hath stretched forth her hands;
   There is no one to comfort her.
   On her neighbours the Lord laid a charge
   To be hostile to Jacob;
   And now is Jerusalem vile
   And abhorrent among them.

18 As for the Lord, He is just;
   For a rebel was I.
   Ye peoples all, hear, I entreat you,
   And look on my sorrow.
   Together my maidens and youths
   Are gone into captivity.

19 I called upon those that had loved me,
   But they have deceived me.
   In the city my priests and mine elders
   Have perished of hunger.[9]
   For bread they searched in their need,
   But their search was in vain.[10]

Lamentations

20 Look, Lord, for distress is upon me,
    And ferment within me.
  Within me my heart writhes with pain,
    That, for playing the rebel,
  The sword dealeth death in the streets,
    In the houses the pestilence.[11]

21 Listen to these my sighs;
    There is no one to comfort me.
  My foes have all heard with delight
    Of the evil Thou wroughtest me,
  Bringing the day Thou proclaimedst[12]
    For all of my sins.

22 Let their wickedness all come before Thee;
    Let *them* fare like me;
  And do even so unto them
    As Thou didst unto me.[13]
  For my sighs are many and many,
    And sore is my heart.

Lament over the Sorrows of Jerusalem

The Divine Judgment and the Inconsolable Sorrow

ii.
1 Alas! How the Lord is beclouding
    The daughter of Zion![1]
  From heaven down to earth He hath hurled
    The glory of Israel.
  In the day of His wrath He remembers
    His foot-stool[2] no more.

2 Without pity the Lord hath engulfed
    All the homesteads of Jacob.

Lamentations

In His wrath He hath torn clean down
All the strongholds of Judah,
Hath hurled to the ground in dishonour
Her king³ and her princes.

3 He hath hewn in the glow of His anger
  All Israel's horn.
  He hath drawn His right hand back
  From the face of the foe.
  Like a fire He is blazing in Jacob,
  Devouring around.

4 His bow He hath bent like a foeman;
  He stands⁴ as for siege.
  All the lovely He slays in the tent
  Of the daughter of Zion.
  He hath poured forth His anger like fire.⁵

5 The Lord hath become like a foe;
  He hath swallowed up Israel,
  Swallowed her palaces all—
  He hath ruined her strongholds,
  And heaped on the daughter of Zion
  Lamenting and woe.

6 His booth like His vine⁶ He hath ravaged;
  He hath ruined His trysting-place.
  Jehovah hath blotted from Zion
  The feast and the sabbath.
  The king and the priest He hath spurned
  In the heat of His anger.

7 The Lord hath rejected His altar
  And cast off His holy place,

Lamentations

    Given to the hands of the foemen
        The walls of her palaces.[7]
    In the house of the Lord there were shouts
        Like the shouts of a feast-day.

8 For the walls of the daughter of Zion
        The Lord hath planned ruin.
    He stretched out the line, and withdrew not
        His ravaging hand.
    Wall and rampart He plunged into mourning—
        Together they languish.

9 Sunk in the dust are her gates,
        And her bars He hath shivered.
    Her king and her princes are exiles
        And guidance[8] is none.
    Yea, and no vision hath come
        From the Lord to His prophets.

10 Speechless they sit on the ground,
        Even the elders of Zion—
    With dust cast up on their heads,
        And with girdles of sack-cloth.
    The maids of Jerusalem bow
        With their heads to the ground.

11 Mine eyes are wasted with weeping,
        My bowels are troubled.
    My heart[9] is poured out on the ground
        For the wreck of my people.
    The babe and the suckling lie faint
        On the streets of the city.

12 To their mothers they keep on saying,
        " O where is our bread ? "

Lamentations

Like the wounded they lie in a swoon
    On the streets of the city,
As they pour out their lives (to the death)
    On the breasts of their mothers.

13 With what shall I rank or compare thee,
    O daughter of Jerusalem ?
Where is thy like, that I comfort thee,
    Virgin of Zion ?
For vast as the sea is thy ruin ;
    (Alas !) who can heal thee ?

14 The visions thy prophets have brought thee
    Are false and dishonest.
They did not uncover thy guilt,
    And so save thee from exile.
The visions they uttered for thee
    Were deceptive and false.

15 They clapped their hands over thee—
    All they that passed by.
They hissed and they wagged their heads
    At Jerusalem's daughter.
" Is this the city men called
    The Perfection of Beauty ? "[10]

16 Against thee thine enemies all
    Opened wide their mouths.
They hissed and they gnashed their teeth :
" We have swallowed her up.
Yes, this is the day that we looked for :
    We have it, we see it."

17 Jehovah hath done what He planned,
    Hath accomplished His word :

Lamentations

As in days long ago He enjoined,
 He hath wrecked without pity,
Hath made thee the sport of thy foes
 And exalted thine enemies.

18 Cry thou aloud to the Lord,
 O virgin of Zion.[11]
Pour down thy tears like a torrent
 By day and by night.
Give to thyself no respite,
 No rest to thine eyes.

19 Arise, pierce the night with thy cries,
 As each night-watch beginneth.
Pour out like water thy heart
 In the face of the Lord.
Lift up thy hands unto Him
 For the life of thy little ones.[12]

20 Behold, O Lord, and consider
 Whom thus Thou maltreatest.
Shall women devour their own offspring,
 The babes that they dandled?
Shall the priest and the prophet be slain
 In the Lord's holy place?

21 In the streets on the ground they are lying—
 The young and the old.
My maidens and young men together
 Are fallen by the sword.
In the day of Thy wrath Thou hast slaughtered
 And slain without pity.

22 Thou didst summon, as though 'twere a feast-day,
 The villages[13] round.

Lamentations

But not one in the day of Thine anger
  Escaped or was left;
The children I brought up and fondled
  Were slain by the foe.

Lament and Prayer[1]

iii.
1 I am the man[2] who was humbled
     By the rod of His anger.
2 The way that He guided and led me
     Was dark and unlighted.
3 Against me alone was His hand
     Ever turned all the day.

4 He hath shrivelled my flesh and my skin;
     He hath broken my bones.
5 He hath built round about me a wall
     Of exhaustion and bitterness.
6 He hath made me to dwell in the darkness
     As those long dead.

7 He hath shut me behind solid walls;
     He hath loaded my chain.
8 When I cry and entreat Him for help,
     He is deaf to my prayer.
9 He hath blocked up my path with hewn stone,
     And my way He hath tangled.

10 He lurketh for me like a bear
      Or a lion in ambush.
11 He chased me aside and He tore me
      And left me forlorn.
12 His bow He bent, and He set me
      As mark for His arrow.

Lamentations

13 Into my reins He hath driven
    The shafts of His quiver.
14 A derision was I to all peoples,
    Their song all the day.
15 To the full did He fill me with bitterness,
    With wormwood He sated me.

16 He hath broken my teeth with gravel,[3]
    And heaped me with ashes.
17 He hath robbed me of peace ; and of weal
    I remember no more.
18 So I said, " My glory is gone
    And my hope in Jehovah."

19 The thought[4] of my woe and my wandering
    Is wormwood and gall.
20 My soul doth for ever recall them,
    And is bowed down within me.
21 Now this I will lay on my heart
    And will therefore take hope—

22 That the love of the Lord is unceasing,
    His pity unfailing.
23 Thy kindness is new every morning
    And great is Thy faithfulness.
24 " The Lord is my portion," I said :
    " I will hope then in Him."

25 Those that wait for the Lord find Him gracious—
    The souls that do seek Him.
26 It is good, then, in silence to wait
    For the help of the Lord.
27 It is good for a man that he carry
    A yoke in his youth.

Lamentations

28 Let him sit all alone and keep silence,
   When[5] *He* hath imposed it.
29 Let him lay his lips low in the dust,
   For perchance there is hope.
30 Let him offer his cheek to the smiter
   And bear all the taunt.

31 For Jehovah will not cast away
   The afflicted[6] for ever.
32 Though He wound, He will yet have compassion—
   His love is so great.
33 He is loth to give sorrow or pain
   To the children of men.

34 When[7] the men of a land, taken prisoner,
   Are crushed under foot :
35 When a man is deprived of his right
   In the face of the Highest :
36 When the cause of a man is subverted :
   Doth not the Lord see ?[8]

37 Where is he that can bring things to pass,
   That the Lord hath not ordered ?
38 Do not evil and good come alike
   From the mouth of the Highest ?
39 Why then should a mortal complain
   When chastised for his sins ?

40 Let us search and examine our ways
   And return to the Lord.
41 Let us lift up our hearts with[9] our hands
   Unto God in the heavens.
42 " *We*[10] have transgressed and rebelled,
   And *Thou* hast not pardoned.

Lamentations

43 Thou hast wrapped Thee in wrath and pursued us,
    And slain without pity ;
44 Hast wrapped Thee around in a cloud
    Which no prayer could pass through.
45 Thou hast made us off-scouring and refuse
    In the midst of the nations.

46 Against us our enemies all
    Open wide their mouths.
47 Fear and the pit are upon us,
    Destruction and ruin."
48 Mine eye runs with rivers of water
    For the wreck of my people.

49 Mine eye poureth down without rest
    And without any respite,
50 Until that Jehovah in heaven
    Look down and behold.
51 Mine eyes are vexed with grief
    For the daughters of my city.[11]

52 They have hunted me sore like a bird—
    Those that groundlessly hate me—
53 Have ended my life in the dungeon
    And cast stones upon me.
54 Waters flowed over my head,
    And I said, " I am lost."

55 From the depths of the dungeon, O Lord,
    Did I call on Thy name ;
56 And my voice Thou didst hear : " O hide not
    Thine ear from my cry."
57 Thou camest the day that I called Thee,
    And badest me fear not.

Lamentations

58 Thou pleddest my cause, O Lord,
   And didst ransom my life.
59 Thou hast seen, Lord, how I am wronged;
   O secure for me justice:
60 For all the revenge Thou hast seen
   That they plotted against me.

61 O Lord, Thou hast heard all the insults
   They plotted against me,
62 The threatenings and plots without ceasing
   Of those that assail me.
63 See how, whether sitting or rising,[12]
   They mock me in taunt-songs.

64 Thou wilt requite them, O Lord,
   For the deeds they have done.
65 Blindness[13] of heart wilt Thou give them—
   Thy curse be upon them!
66 Pursue them in wrath and destroy them
   From under Thy heavens.

Lament over the Sorrows of Jerusalem[1]

The Fate of the People and their Leaders

iv.
1 Alas! How bedimmed is the gold,
   The most pure gold.
   The jewels, so sacred, lie scattered
   At every street corner.[2]

2 The children of Zion, the precious,
   Whose worth is as gold,[3]
   Count, alas! but as earthenware pitchers,
   The work of the potter.

Lamentations

3 Even the monsters give breast
    And they suckle their young ;
   But the daughters of my people are cruel
    As ostriches wild.

4 The tongue of the sucking child cleaves
    To his palate for thirst.
   The children are craving for bread ;
    There is none to dispense it.

5 Those that had feasted on dainties
    Now waste on the streets.
   Those that were nurtured in scarlet
    Lie huddled on ash-heaps.

6 The guilt of my people surpassed
    The transgression of Sodom,
   Whose overthrow came in a flash
    Ere a hand could be wrung.[4]

7 Her princes were purer than snow,
    They were whiter than milk,
   With a skin more ruddy than coral
    And veins like the sapphire.[5]

8 Now blacker than darkness their form—
    On the streets no one knows them :
   Their skin is drawn tight on their bones ;
    It is dry as a stick.

9 Better they that are slain with the sword
    Than that perish with hunger,
   Pining away for the lack[6]
    Of the fruits of the field.

Lamentations

10 The hands of compassionate women
      Have sodden their children.
    Yea, *these* have served them for food
      In the wreck of my people.

11 The Lord hath accomplished His wrath,
      Hath poured out His hot anger,
    And kindled in Zion a fire
      Which devoured her foundations.

12 No kings of the earth had believed,
      And no folk in the world,
    That assailant or foeman could enter
      The gates of Jerusalem.

13 It was all for the sins of her prophets,
      The crimes of her priests,
    Who have shed in the midst of the city
      The blood of the righteous.[7]

14 With the blood-stains upon them they reel
      Like the blind through the streets,
    And they touch with their robes those whom erstwhile
      They could not endure.[8]

15 "Away, ye unclean!"—men adjure them—
    "Away, touch us not!"
    So they stagger and wander around[9]
      With no resting for ever.

16 Jehovah Himself hath dispersed them—
      He careth no more.
    For the priests He hath shown no regard,
      For the prophets[10] no pity.

Lamentations

17 How long did our weary eyes watch
   For the help that was vain !
   Yea, on our watch-tower we watched
   For the nation[11] that saved not.

18 They hunted our steps, that we dared not
   Appear in our streets.
   Our days were cut short and completed ;
   Our end was now come.

19 Swifter were they that pursued us
   Than eagles of heaven.
   Over the mountains they chased us ;
   They ambushed the desert.

20 The breath of our life, God's anointed,[12]
   Was trapped in their toils—[13]
   He of whom we had said, " 'Neath his shade[14]
   We shall live as a nation."[15]

21 Be glad and rejoice in thy home-land,[16]
   O daughter of Edom.
   To thee, too, the cup shall come round ; [17]
   Thou'lt be drunken and naked.

22 O Zion, thy guilt is now blotted :
   Of exile no more !
   But *thy* guilt He shall visit, O Edom ;
   Thy sins are laid bare.

Jerusalem's Sorrow and Prayer for Deliverance[1]
Her Sorrows

v.
1 Bethink thee, O Lord, of our plight ;
  Look and see how Thy folk are insulted.

Lamentations

2   Our home-land is turned unto strangers ;
    Our houses are passed unto aliens.
3   Fatherless orphans are we,
    And our mothers are like unto widows.
4   The water we drink we must buy,
    And our wood becomes ours at a price.
5   The yoke presses hard on our necks ; [2]
    We are weary and never find rest.
6   We have stretched out our hands unto Egypt ;
    To Assyria[3] also, for bread.
7   Our fathers, who sinned, are no more ;
    And their guilt has been borne by *us*.
8   Servants are now our lords ;
    From their hand there is no one to save us.
9   We win bread at the risk of our lives
    From the murderous bands of the desert.
10 Like an oven our skin is aglow
    With the fierce fever-heat of famine.
11 The matrons they ravished in Zion,
    The maids in the cities of Judah:
12 Princes were hanged by their hands,
    And the faces of elders dishonoured.
13 Young men had to carry the mill ;
    Youths fell beneath loads of wood.
14 The elders have ceased from the gate
    And the youths given over their music.
15 The joy of our heart is vanished ;
    Our dancing is turned into mourning.
16 The crown is fallen from our head ;
    Woe, woe unto us !   We have sinned.
17 For this is our heart turned faint,
    For these things our eyes are grown dim—

Lamentations

18 For the mountains of Zion, now waste,
    Over which the jackals roam.

Prayer for Deliverance

19 But Thou, Lord, art seated for ever,
    From age to age, on Thy throne.
20 O why then forget us for ever,
    And leave us for long, long days ?
21 Bring us back to Thee, Lord, let us turn,
    And renew our days as of old ;
22 Unless Thou hast utterly spurned us
    And Thine anger is all too sore.

THE SONG OF SONGS

THE SONG OF SONGS

i.
1   The Song of Songs,[1] which is Solomon's.

The Bride Praises the Bridegroom, modestly depreciates
her own Beauty, and asks where her Bridegroom is
to be found [2]

2 O for a kiss from thy lips :
   Thy caresses are better than wine.
3 Thy perfumes are fine in their fragrance ;
   As perfumes poured forth is thy name :
   And therefore the maidens (all) love thee.

4 Draw me after thee. O let us hasten :
   O king,[3] bring me into thy chamber.
   In thee we will joy and be glad ;
   More than wine shall we praise thy caresses.
   Yes, they are right who love thee.

5 I am dark,[4] but yet comely,
   Ye maids of Jerusalem,
   Like (dark) tents of Kedar,
   Like curtains of Solomon.

6 Eye me not strangely,
   Because I am dark :
   'Tis the sun that hath scorched me.

   Once the sons of my mother
   Were angry with me,
   So they set me to watch the vineyards ;

The Song of Songs

But the vineyard that was mine own[5]
I watched not at all.

7 O tell me, beloved of my soul,
  Where thou restest thy flock at the noon-tide ;
  For why should I wander in vain
  And be found by the flocks of thy comrades ?

8 If[6] thou dost not know at all,
  O thou of women the fairest,
  Go forth on the trail of the flock,
  Feed thy kids where the shepherds are tented.

Bride and Bridegroom sing each other's Praises

Dialogue

9 " I[7] liken thee, O my love,
    To a filly in Pharaoh's chariot—
10 Thy cheeks all lovely with spangles,
    Thy neck with strings of jewels ;
11 And circlets of gold we will make thee
    With pendants of silver."

12 " While the king[8] on his couch[9] is reclining,
    My spikenard yieldeth its fragrance.
13 A scent-bag of myrrh is my loved one,
    That lieth between my breasts.
14 My love is a cluster of henna
    In the vineyards of En-gedi."

15 " O how fair,[10] my love, art thou ;
    How fair, with thy dove-like eyes ! "

16 " O how fair,[11] my beloved, how lovely !
    And green is our bed.

218

The Song of Songs

17 Our house hath cedars for beams,
    And our rafters are fir.

ii.
1 A crocus[1] of Sharon am I,
    A lily of the valleys."

2 "As a lily among the thorns,
    So is my love among the daughters."

3 "As an apple-tree in the forest,
    So is my love among the sons.
    In his shadow I sit with delight,
    And his fruit is sweet to my taste."

The Happiness of the Bride

4 To the house of wine he hath brought me,
    O'erhung with the banner of love.
5 Stay me with cakes of raisins,
    And strengthen me with apples,
    For faint with love am I.

6 His left arm was under my head,
    And his right arm round about me.
7 I adjure you, ye maids of Jerusalem,
    By the roes and the hinds of the field,
    That ye rouse not love[2] nor awake her,
    Until it be her good pleasure.

A Spring Wooing

8 Hark, my beloved!
    See, he cometh,
    Leaping the mountains,
    Skipping the hills.
9 See,[3] there he standeth
    In front of our wall.

The Song of Songs

    I* look from the window,
      I* peer through the lattice ;
10 And thus my beloved
      Makes answer to me.

    " Arise, my beloved,
      My fair, come away.
11 For see ! the winter is past,
      The rain is over and gone,
12 The flowers appear in the land,
      The time for pruning* is come,
    And the voice of the ring-dove is heard.
13 The figs on the fig-trees are reddening,
      The vines are all blossom and fragrance.
    Arise, my beloved,
      My fair, come away.

14 O my dove, from thy craggy retreat,
      From thy hiding-place steep,
    O show me thy face,
      Let me hear thy voice ;
    For thy voice is so sweet
      And thy face is so lovely."

15 Take us the foxes,
      The little foxes,
    That ruin our vineyards,*
      Those blossoming vineyards.

16 My beloved is mine, I am his :
      'Mong the lilies he pastures.

The Song of Songs

17 Till cool grows the day,
    And the shadows depart,
    O turn, my beloved,
    And sport like the roe
    Or the playful gazelle
    On the cleft-riven[7] mountains.

The Bride's Dream

iii.
1 On my bed in the night did I seek
    The beloved of my soul.
    But I sought him in vain.

2 " I will rise and go over the city,
    Its streets and its squares.
    I will seek the beloved of my soul."
    But I sought him in vain.

3 I was met by the watchmen who passed
    On their round of the city.
    (" Tell me," I said), " have ye seen
    The beloved of my soul ? "

4 Scarce had I parted from them
    When I found the beloved of my soul.
    I held him and slacked not my hold,
    Till I brought him home to my mother.[1]

5 I adjure you, ye maids of Jerusalem,
    By the roes and the hinds of the field,
    That ye rouse not love[2] nor awake her
    Until it be her good pleasure.

The Song of Songs

The Bridegroom's Procession

6 What is this that comes up from the desert
    Like columns of smoke,
    Perfumed with myrrh and frankincense,
    All scents of the merchant ?

7 Behold, it is Solomon's litter,
    And round it three score valiant men[3]
    Of the valiant of Israel,
8 Each with a sword in his hand,
    And acquainted with war—
    Every man with a sword on his thigh
    For the terrors of night.

9 The king[4] had a palanquin made him
    Of Lebanon wood.
10 Its feet he had fashioned of silver ;
    Its back was of gold.
    Its seat was of purple : within
    It was inlaid with ebony.[5]

11 Come forth and look on the king,[5]
    Ye daughters of Zion,
    In the crown he received from his mother,
    The day he was wedded
    With gladness of heart.

In Praise of the Charms of the Bride

iv.
1 How fair, my love, art thou,
    With thy dove-like eyes
    Behind thy veil ;
    And thy hair like a flock of goats
        Streaming down from mount Gilead ;

The Song of Songs

2 Thy teeth like a flock new shorn
    Just come up from the washing,
    Ranged in a double row,
    Not one of them lacking ;[1]

3 Thy lips like a scarlet thread,
    And thy mouth so lovely ;
    Thy temples like pieces of pomegranate,
    Seen through thy veil ;

4 Thy neck like the tower of David,
    Built for an armoury,[2]
    Hung with the thousand shields,
    All shields of the valiant ;
5 Thy breasts like a pair of fawns
    That are twins of a roe ![3]

6 Till the day grow cool
    And the shadows depart
    I will go to the mountain of myrrh,
    And the hill of frankincense.[4]
7 O my love, thou art fair altogether ;
    There is no spot in thee.

9 Thou[5] hast ravished me, sister[6] and bride.
    One glance of thine eyes hath bewitched me,
    One glint of thy necklace.[7]
10a How sweet thy caress, sister bride !
10b   How much better than wine thy caresses !

11 Thy lips, O my bride, drip with honey,
    And milk lieth under thy tongue.
    Thy garments are fragrant as Lebanon ;
10c   Thy perfumes are sweeter than balsam.

The Song of Songs

12 A garden enclosed is my sister,
    A garden enclosed, a sealed fountain;
13 Thy shoots are a pomegranate paradise—
    Choicest of fruits,
    Henna and spikenard,
14   Spikenard and saffron,
    Calamus and cinnamon,
      With all trees of incense,
    Aloes and myrrh,
      With the chief spices all.
15 Thou art the fount of my garden,
    A well of fresh water,
    Like streamlets of Lebanon.

16 O North wind, awake,
    And come, thou South,
    And blow on my garden,
    That perfume be wafted.

    " Let[8] my darling come into his garden
    And taste its choice fruits."

v.
1 I am come[1] to my garden, my sister;
    I gather me balsam and myrrh.
    I have tasted the comb with the honey,
    And drunk of my wine and my milk.
    Taste ye, my friends, and drink;
    Yea, drink yourselves drunken, beloved.

In Praise of the Bridegroom
The Bride tells her Tale
2 I slept, but my heart was awake.
    O hark! my beloved is knocking.

The Song of Songs

"Open to me, my sister,
    My dove, my beloved, all spotless.
For wet is my head with the dew,
    And my locks with the drops of the night."

3 "I[2] have laid my garment aside,
    And why should I don it again?
My feet, too, I have washed,
    And why should I soil them again?"

4 My love put his hand through the opening,[3]
    And moved was my heart for him.
5 So I rose to let in my darling:
    My hands were dripping with myrrh,
With the myrrh that ran over my fingers
    And on to the catch of the bolt.

6 I opened the door to my love,
    But my darling had turned and was gone;
And the soul of me sank, when he vanished.[4]
    I sought him, but all in vain:
    I called, but he gave me no answer.

7 The watchmen were tramping the city;
    They met me, they beat me and wounded me.
Those who kept watch on the walls
    Seized the mantle that I had thrown over me.

8 I adjure you, ye maids of Jerusalem,
    If so be ye find my beloved,
What, then, shall ye tell my beloved?
    That faint with love am I.

The Song of Songs

9 " What⁵ is *thy* darling more than another
    O thou of women the fairest ?
    What is *thy* darling more than another,
    That thou dost adjure us so ?"

The Bride's Praise of the Bridegroom
10 " My beloved is radiant and ruddy,
    The chief among ten thousand.
11   His head is finest gold ;
    His curls are as black as the raven.

12   His eyes are like doves
    Over brooklets of water,
    Or bathing in milk,
    As they perch on the brink.⁶

13   His cheeks are like beds of spices,
    Like banks of sweet herbs.
    His lips are like lilies—adrip
    With their liquid myrrh.

14   His arms are like tapers of gold
    That are inlaid with jasper ;⁷
    His belly like ivory wrought
    And encrusted with sapphires.

15   His legs are like pillars of marble
    On sockets of gold.
    He looks altogether like Lebanon,
    Grand as the cedars.

16   Sweetness itself is his mouth ;
    He is all of him lovely.
    Such is my love and my darling,
    Ye maids of Jerusalem."

The Song of Songs

Conclusion

vi.
1 " Whither[1] hath gone thy beloved,
   O fairest of women ?
   Whither hath turned thy beloved,
   That with thee we may seek him ? "

2 " My love is gone down to his garden,
   The terrace of spices,
   To pasture his flock in his garden
   And gather the lilies.
3 My beloved is mine, I am his,
   'Mong the lilies he pastures."

In Praise of the Bride

4 Thou art fair, my beloved, as Tirzah,[2]
   Lovely as Jerusalem,
   Dread as an army with banners.
5 Away from me turn those eyes
   That stir me so strangely,
   That hair like a flock of goats
   Streaming down from mount Gilead.

6 Those teeth like a flock of ewes,
   Just come up from the washing,
   Ranged in a double row,
   Not one of them lacking ;
7 Those temples like pieces of pomegranate
   Seen through thy veil.[3]

8 Three score queens had Solomon,[4]
   Concubines fourscore,
   And maids without number.
9 But she, my dove, is but one,[5]
   She, my stainless, is one.

The Song of Songs

Alone and peerless is she
To the mother who bore her.
The daughters, at sight of her, praised her ;
Concubines, queens, sang her praises.

10　Who is this that looks forth like the dawn,
Fair as the moon,
Clear as the sun,
And dread as an army with banners ?

11 "I went down[6] to the garden of nuts,
To see the green shoots in the valley,
To see if the vines were in bud,
Or the pomegranates yet were in blossom.
12　Or ever I knew, on his chariot
The prince of my people had set me."[7]

13　Turn thee, turn, maid of Shulem,[8]
Turn thee, turn, that we see thee.
But what would ye see in the Shulammite ?
(We would see her dance) the war-dance.[9]

In Praise of the Bride as she dances the Sword-Dance

vii.
1　How gracefully thou dost step
In thy sandals, thou prince's daughter!
The curves of thy thighs are like jewels,
Wrought by the hands of an artist.

2　Thy waist[1] is a rounded bowl—
Be never the sweet wine wanting.
Thy belly a heap of wheat,
That is set about with lilies.

228

The Song of Songs

3 Thy breasts like a pair of fawns
    That are twins of a gazelle,
4 Thy neck like the ivory tower.
    Thine eyes are like Heshbon's pools,
    By the gate of the populous city,[2]

    Thy nose like the tower of Lebanon
    That looketh toward Damascus,
5 Thy head is like Carmel upon thee,
    Thy flowing locks are as purple :
    Thy tresses hold captive the king.

6 How fair, my beloved, art thou !
    How lovely in love's delights !
7 Thou art slender and tall as a palm,
    And thy breasts are like its clusters.

8 I vowed I would climb this palm,
    And take hold of the branches thereof.
    O let thy breasts be as clusters,
    The smell of thy breath be as apples,
9 Thy lips[3] be as wine of the best,
    That goeth down smoothly
    And glides o'er the lips and the teeth.[4]

The Bride's Longing

10 I am my darling's ;
    He longeth for me.
11 Come, then, my love,
    Let us go to the fields,
    Let us lodge among the henna.[5]

12 And early we'll hie to the vineyards,
    To see if the vine be in bud,

The Song of Songs

If its blossoms have opened,
And pomegranates flower ;
And there my caresses I'll give thee.

13 The love-apples give forth their scent ;
At our door are all manner of fruits,
Precious fruits, both new and old,
That I stored up for thee, my beloved.

viii.
1 O that thou wert my brother,
That nursed at the breasts of my mother !
If I found thee without, I would kiss thee,
Nor fear the contempt of another.

2 To my mother's house I would bring thee,
To the chamber of her that conceived me.[1]
Spiced wine would I give thee to drink,
A draught of my pomegranate wine.[2]

The Incomparable Power of Love

5 Who is this that comes up from the wilderness,[3]
Leaning upon her beloved ?

" 'Neath the apple-tree yonder I woke thee,[4]
Just there, where a babe thou wast swaddled[5]—
Yes, there—by the mother that bore thee."

6 " Set me[6] as seal[7] on thy heart
Like the ring on thy hand.

For love is strong as death,
Its passion[8] is fierce[9] as the grave ;[10]
Its flashes are flashes of fire,
Its flames are like the lightning.[11]

The Song of Songs

7   No waters can quench it,
    Nor floods overwhelm it.
    If a man should give all in his house for it,
    Utterly scorned would he be.

The Bride's Proud Reply to her Brothers

8   "A sister have we,[12] but she's little—
    No breasts hath she yet.
    What then shall we do with our sister,
    The day she is spoken for?

9   If she should prove a wall,
    We will build her a turret of silver.[13]
    But if she should prove a door,
    We will fence her with boards of cedar."[14]

10 "I was a wall,
    My breasts were the turrets;[15]
    And he,[16] as he looked at me,
    Won me my happiness."

The Two Vineyards

11 Solomon[17] had a vineyard at Baal-hamon—
    He let out the vineyard to keepers;
    And each man brought in for the fruit thereof
    One thousand shekels of silver.

12 I, too, have a vineyard,[18] mine own:
    I leave thee the thousand, O Solomon;
    Yea, and two hundred besides
        For the men who kept watch on the fruit thereof.

The Song of Songs

Conclusion

13 "O thou that hauntest the gardens,[19]
   My comrades are all attention :
   Come, let us hear thy voice."[20]

14 "Hasten, beloved,
      And flee[21] like the roe
   Or the playful gazelle
      On the mountains of spices."

NOTES

NOTES

JOB

LXX. stands for the Septuagint or Greek version of the Old Testament.

The letters *a, b, (and c)*, stand respectively for the first, second, (and third) of the lines composing a verse.

I. 1 Possibly N.E. of Palestine, in the Hauran; more probably, however, to the south, in the neighbourhood of Edom.

5 The present text reads " blessed "—no doubt a euphemistic alteration of later scribes, in the interests of religious propriety.

6 Lit. " the sons of " (*i.e.*, those who belong to the category of) " the gods " or supernatural beings, of whom Jehovah is chief, as in Ps. xxix. 1. *Cf.* " sons of the prophets " = men of the prophetic order, prophets. The phrase implies ancient mythological conceptions, transcended when the Book of Job was written, but retained (or introduced) as part of the supernatural machinery of the book.

Lit. " *The* Satan," *i.e.*, the Adversary. The word is strictly an epithet, not a proper name, as it afterwards came to be. The Satan is one of the supernatural Beings; and, as such, he reports to his overlord Jehovah.

15 Elsewhere a trading tribe of southern Arabia (*cf.* vi. 19) —here apparently regarded as a robber tribe, hovering on its northern borders.

17 Whether or not these are to be identified with the well-known people of that name in southern Babylonia, they are here, like the Sabeans, regarded as marauders.

21 Satan hopes to hear the word " cursed " (*v.* 11). In the Hebrew the last word—for which the writer skilfully keeps us waiting with bated breath — is *blessed*.

II. 11 Teman in Edom; there were Shuhites on the Euphrates; the site of Naamah is unknown.

Notes

III. 8 The great primeval monster, hostile to and subdued by the God of light at creation. If it is stirred up darkness will again be ushered in.
12 The knees of the father, who thus acknowledges and makes himself responsible for the upbringing of the child.
14 Meaning of this word very uncertain.
22 Such as cover corpses that have no proper grave, *e.g.*, Achan (Joshua vii. 26), Absalom (2 Sam. xviii. 17).

V. 1 *I.e.*, the angels. *Cf.* xv. 15.
3 So LXX.
5 Text and meaning uncertain. Middle clause omitted as apparently variant or duplicate.
7 The sons of flame would be the angels. But the real meaning of the line is quite uncertain.

VI. 6 Or, " in the juice of the purslain "—in either case a figure for insipid discourse.
7 7*b* is omitted as probably an Aramaic gloss to 6*b*.
19 Tema in northern Arabia
For them, *i.e.*, the torrents.
Sheba in southern Arabia.
26 *I.e.*, for winds to carry away.
29 The friends are turning away from him.

VII. 2 The shadow of evening.
9 *I.e.*, the underworld.
12 The primeval dragon (of Babylonian mythology) subdued by the Creator. *Cf.* iii. 8.
17 This looks like a bitter parody of Ps. viii. 4.
19 Lit. " till I swallow my spittle."
20 The Jewish tradition is probably right which takes the original text to be, " And I am become a burden *to Thee*—later altered from motives of reverence to *to myself. Cf.* i. 5.

VIII. 11 *Vv.* 11—19 represent the wisdom of the fathers (8—10).
16 At *v.* 16 the figure changes. The text of *v.* 17*b* is uncertain.

IX. 2 Lit. " how can man *be in the right* " and win his right— facing such a Disputant ?
3 *I.e.*, one question.
5 Lit. " without knowing it " (emended text).
9 Either some constellation is meant, or more probably

Job

the treasure-chambers of the stars in the southern skies.

10 Quoted from Eliphaz in v. 9.

13 The mythical monsters who helped the great primeval dragon in his contest with God at creation.

25 A postal courier.

X. 1 So LXX.

16 Marvellous torments to match the marvel of his creation: bitter irony.

XI. 5 In the sequel God does speak, but it is against the friends xlii. 7; and Job is commended as His servant who has spoken the truth about Him.

6 For "double" A.V. ("manifold," R.V.) by a slight change.

Lit "causes some of thy guilt to be forgotten"; but the text is probably at fault.

8 The underworld.

12 This has a proverbial ring. The assonance is in the Hebrew.

XII. 3 *I.e.*, assertions of the inseparable connection of piety with prosperity, and of sin with misfortune—doctrines in which Job, like his friends, had been trained.

4*f*. These verses are exceedingly obscure.

9 Nowhere else in the genuine speeches does *Jehovah* occur, but always some form of the word for *God, Almighty*, etc. This line reappears also, word for word, in Isa. xli. 20. If it is genuine, the word *God* may have originally stood here, as in some MSS.

23 Or "spreads them out and then carries them off." Meaning uncertain.

XIII. 27 A block fastened on the feet (*e.g.* of captives) to hamper the movement. Omit *my feet* from "the roots of my feet," and read *my roots*.

28 If the text is correct, the complaint here passes from the particular to the general.

XIV. 4 Something may have dropped out after "Not one," which is too short to make a line.

16 So LXX.

XV. 8 Lit. "Didst thou hear in" (practically = belong to) "the council of God?"

237

Notes

11   The consolation Eliphaz had sought to administer in chs. iv. and v., and especially the vision in iv. 12 *ff*.
15   The angels. *Cf*. v. 1.
23   So LXX.
28   So, in general, LXX.
29   So LXX; but the meaning of the verse is exceedingly obscure.
30   The first line of *v*. 30 appears to be a variant of *v*. 22*a*.
31   An unusually obscure verse; the translation rests on emended text. Some regard the verse as a gloss to *v*. 35.

XVI. 3   Allusion to Eliphaz's figure in xv. 2.
15   Figure for utter humiliation.
21   The Friend is God.

XVII. 5   The meaning of this verse is hopelessly uncertain.
7   *Vv*. 8—10 come more naturally after xviii. 3.
10   The second line of *v*. 10—" I can find not a wise man among you "—was perhaps added as the complement to the first, when that had become displaced.
13   Lit. "Sheol." So *v*. 16.

XVIII. 13   Perhaps, though not certainly, an allusion to the leprosy which was devouring Job.
14   Meaning uncertain.
15   Text uncertain: perhaps " Lilith," a night-demon (*cf*. Isa. xxxiv. 14), perhaps " destruction."

XIX. 12   The last clause of the verse, " encamping around my tent," is not in LXX., tends to confuse the metaphor and is metrically superfluous.
17   An almost certain emendation for the " supplication " of the text. It is a strong expression, occurring again in Joel ii. 20.

    Lit. " the children of my body." But, as Job's children were dead (i. 19), some suppose either that the poet for the moment has overlooked this, or that he does not trouble about the details of the story. Others, with much less probability, think that the reference is to children by concubines, others to members of Job's clan, others again to his brothers— children of his (mother's) womb.

20   " Flesh " should apparently be transferred to the second line to replace the word " skin."

Job

25 Lit. "my vindicator." The word does not mean redeemer (from sin), but vindicator.

26 It is deeply to be regretted that the text of this immensely important passage (*vv*. 25—27) is extremely uncertain. Without emendation no real sense can be made of the words rendered by R.V. "hath been thus destroyed." Two simple changes, one of which has the indirect support of LXX., give the words Witness and Sponsor, which bring the passage into striking connection with xvi. 19, and produce a remarkably fine climax.

27 The first clause of *v*. 27, "whom I shall see for myself" (A.V., R.V.) or "on my side" (Amer. R.V.), consists of letters so similar to the last clause of *v*. 26 that one is driven to suspect that it (*i.e.*, 27*a*) should be deleted as due to dittography. This has the additional advantage of securing a verse of normal length. See my *Problem of Pain*, pp. 127—136.
Lit. "reins." He faints apparently with rapture at the vision of his Vindicator.

29 *I.e.*, divine wrath.
The last clause should perhaps be deleted. It is metrically superfluous and its meaning is disputed—"that ye may learn that there is a Judge" or "judgment," or "that ye may learn to know the Almighty."

XX. 7 Lit. "his dung."
10 Both lines of this verse are very obscure.
18 Emended text: verse very obscure.
23 As three-line verses are very rare in Job, if indeed they occur at all, some scholars are inclined to omit the first line of *v*. 23.
27 This verse is the answer to Job's assertion and appeal in xvi. 18*f*.

XXI. 2 Sarcastic allusion to xv. 11.
4 Alas! it is not man but God Himself.
17 As Bildad had maintained in xviii. 5.
19 This is the orthodox answer to Job's indignant challenge that the wicked prosper.
28 Job himself is the ungodly tyrant.
33 Omit the third line of the verse.

Notes

34 Job ends as he began. *Cf. v.* 2.

XXII. 8 Lit. "his home." Job, of course, is the strong unscrupulous man of rank.

16 The reference is apparently to the story of the Flood.

19 "Men who said unto God, ' O leave us ;
What can the Most High do unto us ? '
Though He filled their houses with good :
Far from us are the plans of the wicked."
These verses (17*f.*) interrupt the context, and are little more than a repetition of lines in xxi. 14—16.

23 So LXX.

30 For " island " of A.V. or " not " of R.V. read " man " by the addition of a single letter to the Hebrew.

XXIII. 2 Perhaps a hint that the discussion is to be considered as occupying several days.
So LXX.

6 Formerly Job had maintained that He would ; this is his argument in ch. ix.

7 So LXX.

9 Lit. " on the left."
Lit. " on the right."

12 So LXX.

13 Omit *v.* 14, which is not in LXX. : the first line is obscure.

XXIV. 1 Lit. " Why are times not laid up from (= by) the Almighty ? "
I.e., His *judgment* day.

2 The last verse of the chapter (*v.* 25) suggests that it contained a fierce and seemingly unanswerable challenge of the moral order. In its present form, however, it is harmless enough—a few descriptive sketches of certain outcasts and malefactors. Some scholars therefore believe it to be a later pious substitute for a too audacious original.
So LXX.
So LXX.

5 *Vv.* 5—12 (except perhaps *v.* 9) : a description of wretched pariahs living in the wilderness. The meaning is often very uncertain.

12 So LXX.

Job

13 *Vv.* 13—17 describe malefactors who do their business in the night. The fact that these verses are of three lines each is held by some to strengthen the suspicion of the authenticity of the passage.

17 Text and meaning of *v.* 17 extremely uncertain.

18 An allusion perhaps to the swift light reed boats (ix. 26) of the Nile.

Vv. 18*b*—24 describe some notorious malefactor, but quite in the spirit of the friends. This fact together with the *three*-lined verses (*cf.* note on *v.* 13) tends to confirm the suspicion of their authenticity. The verses are obscure to the point of desperation. Duhm's reconstruction has, in the main, been followed.

22 For " mighty " LXX. reads, by a very slight change, " perishing," *i.e.*, (financially) ruined.

24 So LXX.

XXV. 2 *I.e.*, among rebellious angels in heaven. How much more must He be able to rule on earth !

3 So LXX.

XXVI. 2 It is fairly certain that chs. xxv. and xxvi. ought both to be given to Bildad. Notice the new beginning in ch. xxvii., which would be unnecessary if ch. xxvi. were really Job's. The real beginning of Bildad's speech is probably in xxvi. 2. In its present place ch. xxv. hangs in the air.

The weak and strengthless one is God. According to Bildad, Job has been maintaining that God has neither the strength nor the wisdom to rule the world properly.

5 Prehistoric rebellious giants, defeated by God and thrust down to Sheol.

6 The place of destruction or ruin : synonymous with, or part of, Sheol (the underworld).

12 The great primeval dragon of Babylonian myth. *Cf.* ix. 13.

13 Leviathan ; see iii. 8.

XXVII. 1 This, no doubt the original introduction, was altered to " again took up his parable, and said," after the previous chapter had been erroneously ascribed to Job.

7 Lit. " let him become." It is as good as certain that this whole passage (*vv.* 7—23, except *v.* 12), which is exactly in the tone of the friends, should be assigned

Notes

to Zophar, who otherwise would have no place in the third cycle of speeches. Note the resemblance between v. 13 and xx. 29 which is Zophar's.

10 So LXX.
12 This verse appears to be the conclusion of Job's speech, which, it is believed, was suppressed as too bold and irreverent an attack on the divine government of the world.
15 *I.e.*, not by men : practically = they lie unburied.
16 Figure for abundance.
22 One : possibly *men*, more probably *God*.
23 In heaven.

XXVIII. It is generally believed that this fine description of Wisdom (which will be found on pp. 92f.) is not integral to the book. It does not connect well either with the preceding or following chapter. The serenity that breathes through this chapter would not naturally be followed by the lamentations of ch. xxix., and it would further be dramatically inappropriate for a man in agony to speak thus didactically.

1 If the poem originally began, as Duhm supposes, with the refrain (*cf. vv.* 12, 20) the *for*, with which it now begins, is very naturally explained.
3 Metre seems to demand one or two slight omissions.
4 Much in this verse is very uncertain. *Vv.* 3—11 describe mining operations.
8 *I.e.*, wild beasts.
19 *I.e.*, Ethiopia.
22 *Cf.* note on xxvi. 6.

XXIX. 1 This, no doubt the original introduction, was altered to " again took up his parable, and said," after the intrusion of xxviii. *Cf.* xxvii. 1.
6 Or more strictly " curd."
18 A reference perhaps to the fabled phœnix which, after a life of five hundred years, was said to burn itself in its nest and rise again from its ashes.
21 As *vv.* 11*ff.* interrupt, while *vv.* 21—25 continue the description of Job in the assembly, these verses should perhaps be transferred to this point, where they are peculiarly appropriate.
25 The last clause in the existing text of this verse probably stood originally at the end of *v.* 24.

Job

XXX. *Vv.* 2—8 appear to be an independent poem, describing outcasts of the type sketched in xxiv. 5—8 (or 12), and *v.* 1 (which is so very different in tone from Job's magnanimous words in xxxi. 15) may have been added to introduce the passage. The whole is as follows :—

1 But now I am mocked by men
  Whose days number less than mine own—
  By men whose fathers I spurned
  To set with the dogs of my flock.
2 Yea, the strength of their hands is faint,
  Vigour is perished within them.
3a They are shrivelled with want and hunger.
3b They gnaw the herbs of the desert,
4 Mallows they pluck by the bushes,
  And the roots of the broom are their meat.
3c They grope in the waste of the wilderness,
5 Driven from the haunts of men
  With shouts, as one shouts at a thief.
6 In awesome valleys they dwell,
  In holes of the earth and the rocks ;
7 Among the bushes they bray,
  Under the nettles they couple,
8 Sons of the fool and the nameless,
  Scourged right out of the land.

With the braying of *v.* 7 *cf.* the " wild asses " of xxiv. 5.

The text of the passage is in places uncertain and the meaning obscure.

11 Reversing the situation of xxix. 20*b*.
   Text of 11*b* uncertain: but this would be apparently an allusion to xxix. 25.
12 Text uncertain : the figure is that of a siege.
14 Text and meaning of *vv.* 13*f.* exceedingly obscure. The emended text rests in part on LXX.
18 So Duhm.
21 So LXX.
22, 24, 28 Emended text.
28 *I.e.*, howling—with reference to their cries : emended text.

XXXI. 1 So Peake, for the " virgin " of the text which, besides anticipating *vv.* 9*f.*, seems too specific at this point.

Notes

2 Lit. " What would He *assign* . . . and *allot?* "
11 Lit. " judges "—*i.e.*, calling for trial and punishment by human judges.
12 *Cf.* note on xxvi. 6
15 Here, as elsewhere in the chapter (*cf. vv.* 38—40) the verses appear to be dislocated a little. At any rate they gain by the transposition.
18 By a necessary change in the pointing. *He, i.e.,* God.
21 By an exceedingly slight but necessary change. The fatherless have already been dealt with in *v.* 17.
23 This verse is difficult to place: some place it after *v.* 14.
26 Lit. " light "—primarily the sun, but probably intended to include the stars, etc. The reference is to the worship of the heavenly bodies.
28 Like adultery. *Cf. v.* 11.
33 By an extremely slight change, for " like Adam." The text adds " by concealing my guilt in my bosom," which seems superfluous, metrically and otherwise.
35 = signature.
38 These verses (38—40) are almost certainly misplaced, though opinions differ as to where in the chapter they should come.
39 Lit. " eaten."
XXXII. It is almost universally agreed that the speeches of Elihu (xxxii.—xxxvii.) which will be found on pp. 80—91, are a later addition to the book. In the most unfortunate way they mar the splendidly dramatic transition from the challenge with which Job had concluded his great speech (xxxi. 35—37) to the appearance of Jehovah in the storm with which that challenge is answered (xxxviii.). Further, Elihu is completely ignored not only in the prologue, but also in the epilogue (xlii. 7). His speeches add little that is new to the discussion. The literary art of the section is, speaking generally, inferior to that of the rest of the book. It is imitative rather than creative. The speeches, in all probability, are an orthodox addition to the book from the pen of some later scholar who was offended by Job's accusations of God and protestations of his own innocence.

Job

3   There was a Jewish tradition that *God* should be read here instead of *Job*. " They condemned *God* "—this was the effect, though not the intention, of their futile speeches.
6   This word (more literally *knowledge*) is a favourite with Elihu. *Cf. vv.* 10, 17, etc.
8   By a very slight change.
13 Manifestly a (later) polemic against the divine speeches (xxxviii*ff.*). There is no need, Elihu argues, for divine intervention.
15—17 The reference to the silence of the friends takes the form of a soliloquy, as if he ignored their presence.
21 *I.e.*, I will be impartial.

XXXIII. 12 Translation of verse rests on emended text.
15 God's first manner of speech—by a vision of night—is described in *vv.* 15—18.
Quotation from Eliphaz, iv. 13*b*.
16 Rests in part on LXX.
17 So LXX.
18 Simple emendation.
19 God's second manner of speech (19*ff.*)—by sickness.
24 *I.e.*, to the death-angel.

XXXIV. 3 This assonance, though not in the Hebrew, not unfairly represents Elihu's style.
20 By the addition of a single letter to the word for "people."
Lit. " without (stroke of) hand."
23 Most of the verses from this point to the end of the chapter are extremely obscure. The text is highly uncertain and the translation largely conjectural.
30 Lit. "that one of them that ensnare (or pervert) the people may not reign "—*the godless man* being a gloss to explain who the ensnarers or perverters are.
33 Some scholars emend *I* to *God* :—" thou forsooth hast to choose—not God ! "
36 LXX. is nothing like so harsh.
" Howbeit, Job, be admonished (*lit.* learn) ;
Answer no more like the fool."
37 The second clause of the verse, here omitted, is quite obscure.

Notes

XXXV. 10 It is not a cry for God, but only for release from pain.

12 The pride *of their wickedness* (*i.e.*, their wicked pride) rather than *of evil men*—by a very slight textual change.

XXXVI. 5 Read "hard of heart" (by a slight change) for " mighty of understanding," and omit some words as due to dittography.

11 The added clause "and their years in pleasures," which is against the rhythm, is probably a gloss.

16 A hopelessly obscure verse. Duhm's suggestions have been followed.

18—20 These verses are hopelessly difficult and obscure. The ransom is the suffering to be endured, and the intensity of it is not to deflect Job, *i.e.*, turn him aside, from paying it.

30 " Vapour " for " light "—by a very slight change.

31 " Sustaineth " or " feedeth " for " judgeth "—by a very slight change. The reference is to the fructifying power of the rain.

33 Text and meaning very uncertain.

XXXVII. 5 By a simple change, for "thunders." The thunder-scene is over in *v.* 4, and new wonders are introduced by *v.* 5. Omit " with His voice."

7 *I.e.*, indoors.

13 Text and meaning very uncertain.

16 The text " the wonders of Him who is perfect in knowledge " is improbable in view of the context (*cf.* 14*b*) and the parallelism.

20 Emended text.

XXXVIII. 4—38 These verses deal with the inanimate world.

14 The consequence of the sudden rush of light upon the world is that
" From the wicked their light is withheld,
  And the arm that was lifted is broken "(*v.* 15).
The " light " of the wicked is the darkness in which they operate. The couplet seems hardly relevant in an account of creation, when as yet there were no wicked.

17 So LXX.

Job

24 The translation of this verse rests on two very slight textual changes.
31 Exact meaning uncertain: emended text.
32 Mazzaroth. Meaning uncertain: the signs of the zodiac? or some particular star or constellation? Or " Dost thou comfort the Bear for her young?" —perhaps some astro-mythological allusion.
34 So LXX.
36 The meaning of both these words is very uncertain. Possibly a reference to the prognostication of storms.
39 The animate world is dealt with in xxxviii. 39—xxxix. 30, as the inanimate in xxxviii. 4—38.
41 The unpointed text can mean either *for the raven* or *at evening*. Against the former rendering may be urged (i.) that the more natural place for the raven would be beside the hawk and the eagle (xxxix. 26*ff.*); and (ii.) that these two descriptions (if there are two) would be shorter than those of the other birds and animals. Of course these reasons are not absolutely decisive.

XXXIX. 10 So LXX.
13 Text and meaning of verse are disputed.
18 Text and meaning uncertain.
19 Meaning of this word very uncertain.
24 Emended text.
27 By a very simple and probable addition (Budde).

XL. 2 As *v.* 2 continues Jehovah's speech, *v.* 1 ("Jehovah answered Job and said") should probably be omitted.
8 *V.* 8 continues Jehovah's speech, which appears to have originally concluded with *v.* 14. *Vv.* 3—5 (see p. 76) introduce Job's reply which is continued and concluded in xlii. 2—6. *V.* 6 (" Then Jehovah answered Job out of the whirlwind and said " = xxxviii. 1) was added to introduce the conclusion of Jehovah's speech, after it had been interrupted by the premature insertion of part of Job's reply (*vv.* 3—5); and *v.* 7 is but a repetition of xxxviii. 3.
15 The descriptions of the hippopotamus (xl. 15—24; see p. 94) and the crocodile (xli.; see pp. 94*f.*) probably formed no part of the original book. In defence of these passages it is urged that, as the earlier speeches of God (xxxviii*f.*) were to convince

Notes

Job of his ignorance, so these are to convince him of his impotence. But the descriptions, though fine in their way, hardly stand on the same literary level as those of xxxviii*f*.; *cf*. the brief but intensely living pictures of the war-horse (xxxix. 19*ff*.) or the wild ass (xxxix. 5*ff*.). It is hardly probable that these long descriptions, rather unnecessarily retarding, as they do, the crisis between Jehovah and Job for which the sympathetic reader is impatiently waiting, are original to the book.

Usually considered to be the hippopotamus.

19 Emended text: the traditional text is scarcely intelligible.
20 For " play " —by an extremely slight change.

XLI. 1 Leviathan is usually considered here to be the crocodile —(unlike iii. 8).
9 The hope of securing him (*i.e.*, if we emend "*his* hope " to " *thy* hope "). But the text, meaning, and relation of the verse to the context are very uncertain. Some think that the verse is misplaced, and ought to follow xl. 24.
12 The text of the verse is disputed. The *I* is rather inappropriate in a speech of Jehovah.
25 Emended text.
33 Or, by a slight emendation, " Who was made to be lord of the beasts."
34 Rather than " Everything that is high he beholdeth." In Hebrew the verbs for *fear* and *see* are much alike.

I.e., the wild beasts. *Cf*. xxviii. 8.

XLII. 2 This is the natural and no doubt original continuation of Job's speech begun in xl. 4*f*. and interrupted, in our present text, by part of the speech of Jehovah.
3 The line 3*a* is a quotation from xxxviii. 2 ; also 4*b* from xxxviii. 3*b* ; and 4*a* (" Hear, I beseech Thee, and I will speak ") has apparently been added to complete the couplet.

PROVERBS

I. 7 Or " beginning " (or " essence "). *Cf.* ix. 10.
   9 *I.e.*, the instruction and teaching.
  11 For " blood "—by the change of a letter, justified by the parallelism (" innocent ").
  12 Lit. " Sheol."
  15 Omit, with LXX., " my son."
  17 *V.* 16 is not found in the best MSS. of LXX.: it appears to be a gloss from Isa. lix. 7.
" For their feet run to evil,
They haste to the shedding of blood."
  21 So LXX.
  23 Better, in this context, than " pour out my spirit "—though " mine anger " would be possible.
  27 " When distress and anguish come upon you"—apparently a gloss to explain the figure.
  32 Lit. " turning away " (*i.e.*, from Wisdom), refusal to listen to her call.

II. 6 Hebrew " from His *mouth* "; LXX. " from His *face.*"
  9 Simple emendation, for " equity," rectitude.
  16 This and the corresponding word in the next line (frequent words in the Book of Proverbs) mean respectively *strange* and *alien ;* and they—especially the second word—are taken by some to imply that these dissolute women were foreigners. But in this Book the words are practically = harlot or adulteress.
As well as from the wicked man (*v.* 12).
Wisdom.
  17 *I.e.*, her husband.
  20 Lit. " in order that." This summarises the aim of the whole admonition, though it is difficult to reproduce the particle, without clumsiness, in the translation. Toy places the verse after *v.* 9, where it connects naturally and easily.

III. 2 Lit. " length of days and years of life," which, in the Old Testament, usually implies life with God's favour —happy life.
Peace—primarily outward rather than inward.
  3 The last clause, " Write them on the tablet of thy

Notes

heart," which is not in LXX., has apparently been introduced from vii. 3*b*.

4 By a slight change, for " good *understanding.*"
8 So LXX., with very slight change, for " navel."
10 So in part LXX., with change of a single letter.
11 Lit. " loathe."
12 Instead of " as a father "—by an extremely simple change, supported by the parallelism and LXX. (" He scourgeth ").
18 Lit. " a tree of life," a phrase (occurring several times in *Proverbs*: *cf.* xi. 30 ; xiii. 12 ; xv. 4) intentionally reminiscent of the story in Gen. ii.*f.*, but practically = life (idea of *tree* almost obliterated).
23 *I.e.*, against a stone. (*Cf.* Ps. xci. 12).
24 So LXX.
25 Or, " shalt fear not the terror that falls *on the simple ones.*"
27 Emended text. LXX. " the needy." The translation " from them to whom it is due " is slightly questionable.

IV. 5 The line " forget not, and do not decline from the words of my mouth," is metrically superfluous, and does not come naturally before " Do not forsake *her* " (*v.* 6), which implies that *wisdom* has immediately preceded.
6 Verse 7 is not in LXX. The first clause is practically untranslatable. It cannot mean " Wisdom is the principal thing, therefore get wisdom " ; and it can hardly mean " The beginning of wisdom is, Get (or *to* get) wisdom." The second clause means " In all thy substance (or with all that thou hast gotten) buy wisdom."
13 LXX. rather better, " *my* instruction."
17 Or the meaning may be that crime and cruelty are their meat and drink.
19 So LXX. (for Hebr. *as*) by extremely slight change.
23 Lit. " For out of it (not *the heart*, but *the vigilant guarding* of the heart) are the issues to life."

V. 2 Emended in accordance with ii. 11, and with the omission of " thy lips," which is here rather irrelevant, and may have crept in from the next verse. So Toy.
3 Lit. " strange woman." See note on ii. 16.

Proverbs

6 Or " without her perceiving it."
7 So LXX. (" son ").
9 Lit. " glory, splendour " ; but hardly = youthful bloom, for the " others " are *men* (*masc*. pl. ending). This may refer to the punishment of death for adultery (*cf.* Lev. xx. 10 ; Deut. xxii. 22*ff*.), as the first clause may imply that the husband was bought off. Or it may mean " (the toil of) thy years " and so = wealth.
 The husband? Or the creditor of the profligate young man ? Or a slight change would give the word " aliens " as at end of *v*. 10.
11 LXX. " repentest," by a very slight change.
14 *I.e.*, only just escaped conviction and punishment by death at their hands for adultery.
16 So LXX.
18 So LXX. : Hebrew, " blessed."
19 Lit. " intoxicate thee."
20 See note on ii. 16.

VI. 1 See note on *v*. 20. For *vv*. 1—5 on suretyship. *Cf.* xi. 15 ; xvii. 18 ; xx. 5 ; xxii. 26 ; xxvii. 13.
3 Meaning uncertain.
5 By a simple change ; or by the addition of a word, " from the hand (of the hunter.) "
10f. = xxiv. 33*f*.
11 Lit. " wayfarer " (= highwayman).
12 Lit. " depraved " (or a knave) " is the wicked man."
13 Either " speaks with," or (from another root) " rubs, scrapes, shuffles "—supported by two Greek versions, (Aquila and Symmachus).
16 For such arithmetical enumerations, *cf.* xxx. 15—31 Amos, i. 3, 6, 9, 11, 13 ; ii. 1, 4, 6.
20 *Vv*. 1—19, which interrupt the discourse on immorality and have little affinity with the section chs. 1—ix., may have originally belonged to some other section of the book—Toy suggests xxii. 17—xxiv. 34 or xxx. 11—31. At any rate they have the effect of an interpolation where they now stand.
22 Lit. " she."
24 So LXX., by a change of vowels, for " the evil woman."

Notes

26 Slightly emended text: meaning of line not quite certain.
The harlot and the adulteress (lit. married woman) may be the same, in which case the first line may be rendered—though this is very questionable—as in A.V. or R.V.: but vii. 10 furnishes ground for distinguishing the two.

30 By addition of a single letter. Better than " men do not."

31 Or " *will* pay," is ready to pay, *i.e.*, to have silence preserved.

VII. 6 So LXX. and Syriac: Hebrew, " my " and " I " (So v. 7.) But " *her* house " in v. 8 appears to imply that the woman has already been mentioned.

10 Meaning very obscure. With secret (= wily?) heart? with anxious heart? or wakeful (*i.e.*, excited).

11 Lit. " rebellious, stubborn, unruly " (*i.e.*, defying the restraints of shame and breaking the bonds of marriage).

14 Lit. " sacrifices of peace-offerings are with me " or " due from me." The meat which had to be consumed on the day of being offered (Lev. vii. 16) explains and furnishes the entertainment.

19 So LXX.: Hebrew, " the man "—perhaps contemptuously.

22 So LXX.: Hebrew, " suddenly."
So LXX.: the Hebrew is meaningless. Toy, by slight changes, renders; " like a calf that is led to the stall."

24 So LXX. (" son.")

VIII. 3 In the publicity (*vv.* 1—3) and healthfulness (4*ff.*) of her invitation, Wisdom is a fine foil to the stealthy (vii. 12), poisonous (vii. 16—20), and deadly (vii. 22*f.*) appeal of the woman of ch. vii.

6 So LXX.

7 So LXX.: Hebrew, " wickedness."

9 Lit. " straight-forward."

12 " Possess " or " understand " by simple emendations. Hebrew reads " dwell in."

14 *V.* 13 interrupts the context and seems to be an interpolation. It runs thus :—

Proverbs

" The fear of the Lord is the hatred of evil,
    Of arrogance, pride, and the wicked way,
    And the mouth that is perverse I hate."

16 So LXX.
18 Lit. "eminent, glorious (or ancient? durable?) wealth and righteousness "—in the sense of the *prosperity* which is the evidence and the divine seal of righteousness. *Cf.* Ps. cxii. 3.
20 The way of fair play, justice, as explained by *v.* 21.
22 Lit. "as (or *at*) the beginning of His ways," *i.e.*, His ways in creation.

So LXX. Or "possessed." Some Greek versions, however, read "possessed," which in Greek resembles the word for "fashioned."

29 *V.* 29*b*, "that the waters should not transgress His command," is metrically superfluous and may be an explanatory gloss based on Job, xxxviii. 11.
30 The meaning "master-workman," which is really unsupported, is opposed to the whole spirit of the passage, which throughout represents *Jehovah* as creator (*vv.* 26—29) and Wisdom as a *child* born (24*f.*), growing up, and playing (30*f.*).
33 The addition of some such noun seems metrically necessary.

IX. 1 The two women, Wisdom (*vv.* 1—6) and Folly (*vv.* 13—18), with their invitation and appeal, are here contrasted, like the two women in ch. vii. and ch. viii., except that while in vii. 6—23 the woman was a typically immoral woman, here (ix. 13—18) she is rather Folly personified. The obvious relation between the passages suggests that immorality is the supreme folly.

So LXX., by a very slight change, for "hewn."

4 For "she": by a very simple change supported by the LXX. of *v.* 16.
7 This group of aphorisms in *vv.* 7—12 which breaks in between the obviously companion pictures of Wisdom and Folly, has little in common with chs. i.—ix., and would more naturally fit into one of the other sections of the Book. *Cf.* vi. 1—19.

Emended by some to "shame, disgrace" (= insult of *a*).

253

Notes

9 *I.e.*, instruction.
10 *Cf.* i. 7.
11 This verse (in the *first* person) does not fit into the aphorisms of the context in *vv.* 7—12.
12 *I.e.*, the consequences.
13 So LXX.
16 Her invitation begins exactly like that of her counterpart (*v.* 4), which makes the difference between them all the more striking.
18 Lit. " the Shades." *Cf.* ii. 18 ; xxi. 16.

X. The proverbs in this collection (x. 1—xxii. 16) are in couplet form ; *i.e.*, each verse, consisting of two lines, generally exhausts a thought.
6 So LXX. (" of the Lord ").
   This line, as it stands in the Hebrew, does not make a proper antithesis, and should perhaps be altered, as in the translation.
   So LXX.
   By the addition of a single letter to the word for " mouth."
7 Or, by a simple change which gives a better antithesis, " shall be accursed." *Cf.* xi. 26.
9 By a simple change for " shall be known."
10 *Cf.* vi. 13.
   So LXX., which makes an admirable antithesis. The line, as it stands in the Hebrew, repeats *v.* 8*b* and yields no proper antithesis.
13 To drive him on, like the mule. *Cf.* xxvi. 3; Ps. xxxii. 9.
15*a* = xviii. 11*a*.
16 Or " death," by a simple change (instead of " sin ").
18 So LXX.
23 So Toy, who reads " abomination " for " wisdom."
32 By a simple change, for " know."

XI. 1 *Cf.* xx. 10, 23.
4 *I.e.*, God's wrath.
7 LXX., " When a *righteous* man dieth, his hope doth not perish," makes a better antithesis ; but the two lines may be doublets.
8 *Cf.* xxi. 18.

14 The first line shows that the general maxim, as it appears in the second line, is intended to have this particular application.
15 *Cf.* vi. 1—5; xvii. 18.
16 The two bracketed lines are inserted from LXX. The second line of *v.* 16, as it stands in the Hebrew (and English) texts, presents no real antithesis.
 So LXX. (" manly "), by the change of a letter—a change which is almost certainly correct. The Hebrew reads " violent " ; but riches in *Proverbs* are a divine reward, and do not go to the violent.
17 Lit. " his flesh," parallel to (and practically =) " his soul," *i.e.* himself, of the first line.
19 Hebrew = either " so " or " he that is steadfast in." LXX. by the addition of a *tittle* reads " the son of." Emended by some to a participle, meaning " he who is associated with," corresponding to " he who pursues " in *b*.
21 Lit. " hand to hand " ; probably = my hand upon it (assuredly).
 Lit. " the *seed* of the righteous," here = race, not posterity.
23 *I.e.*, God's wrath. *Cf. v.* 4.
27 By a simple change, for " seek."
 " He who seeks evil, it will come upon him."— double meaning of evil, *wrong*, and *disaster*.
28 By the change of a single letter, for *"* fall " : makes better contrast with *b*.
30 Lit. " a tree of life." See note on iii. 18.
 So LXX.
 The phrase rendered in A.V. and R.V. by " *he that winneth souls* " really refers to the *taking of life* (*cf.* i. 19); and for " wise " LXX. suggests " violence."

XII. 6 *I.e.*, the wicked, by calumny in the courts, bring the innocent into peril of their lives.
 Omit *them* : *i.e.*, have a delivering, saving power : or the *them*, if retained, will refer to innocent victims.
9 Or, by a very slight change, a man who is despised because *he works his own field*.
10 Here probably in its original physical, rather than its more common derivative, meaning of " pity."

Notes

11 Lit. "is lacking in *bread*" (using the first two letters of the next verse), for "is lacking in *sense*." *Cf.* xxviii. 19.

12 Omitting the word rendered in A.V. and R.V. by "desireth," which has already been drawn into the last word of v. 11.
By a simple change, for the impossible "yieldeth (fruit)."

14 Frankenberg proposes to omit "good," thus generalising the statement as in second line and as in the very similar xviii. 20.

16 Lit. "on the (very) day." *Cf.* LXX.

26 So Toy, by the change of one letter and the omission of another. The text, as it stands, is hopeless: "the righteous explores ... his neighbour," or, by a change of vowels, "explores his *pasture*: *cf.* Job. xxxix. 8.

27 Meaning extremely uncertain : others, "will not *start* or *roast* his game" (*i.e.*, what he took in hunting). Transpose "precious" and "diligent" in the Hebrew text.

28 Instead of "no death" (= immortality?) we must certainly translate "*to* death." Further, "the way of *the path*" is almost certainly wrong : for *path* some such word as *wickedness* is demanded by the sense.

XIII. 1 By addition of a single letter to word for "father." *Cf.* xii. 1.

2 So LXX., with a good contrast between first and second lines. The Hebrew reads, "from the fruits of his mouth a man enjoys good."

4 Or "shall flourish" : lit. "shall be made fat." Same word as in xi. 25 : xxviii. 25.

6 Or "wickedness overturneth the sinner."

8 This line has little, if any, meaning. R.V. translates "the poor heareth no *threatening* (so LXX.), *e.g.*, from assailants, because he has nothing to be robbed of. This translation is improbable, especially in the light of the similar line xiii. 1*b*. It appears to be a (perhaps accidental) repetition of that line, with the change of "scoffer" to "poor" (each word consisting of only two letters in the Hebrew).

Proverbs

9 So LXX. ("continually") for "Hebrew rejoices."
10 Or, perhaps, by a transposition of consonants " with the *humble* (modest) is wisdom " (as in xi. 2), which makes a better parallelism.
11 So LXX.
12 " A tree of life " : see note on iii. 18.
13 Probably of God. So LXX.
14 *Cf.* xiv. 27.
15 So LXX.
17 For " wicked " read " bad," *i.e.*, bad *as a messenger*. Lit. " brings down into disaster," *i.e.*, those who send him, or his enterprise.
21 So LXX.: also makes good antithesis.
23 The meaning of this couplet is hopelessly obscure. LXX. is altogether different.

XIV. 1 Or possibly, " Wisdom buildeth the house, Folly teareth it down (with her hands)." But such a personification would be more in the spirit of chs. i.—ix. than of x.—xxix.
3 Lit. " a sprig of pride." But " sprig " may mean " rod " as in Aramaic, and in easy emendation gives " back " for " pride." *Cf.* x. 13.
4 By a simple change. This makes a better antithesis than the " crib is *clean* " or " *empty* " — which meanings are unsupported.
7 So Toy. Text very uncertain.
8 So LXX.
9 So Frankenberg. But the text is desperate.
12 = xvi. 25.
14 So LXX. by the addition of a letter.
16 So LXX. (" mixes with "). Hebrew, " bears himself insolently."
17 So LXX. (" bears much "), dropping one letter from the Hebrew, which means " a malicious man is hated."
24 Based on LXX. ; for " their riches." By a slight but necessary change for "folly."
25 By a very slight and probable change for " deceit."
27 *Cf.* xiii. 14.
30 *Cf.* Song of Songs viii. 6. Or " envy, jealousy."

Notes

      31 *Cf.* xvii. 5.
      32 So LXX. (for " in his death ") by transposition of two consonants.
      33 So, Toy. Some such emendation seems necessary.

XV. 4 Lit. " a tree of life." *Cf.* note on iii. 18.
      7 Or, by two simple changes, " The lips of the wise *preserve* (or *observe*) knowledge, But the mind of fools *lacketh insight*."
      11 *I.e.*, generally, the world of the dead: *cf.* note on Job xxvi. 6.
      12 So LXX., for " to."
      19 The LXX. word here is the same as in x. 4*b*, where it represents the Hebrew word for " diligent."
      20 *Cf.* x. 1.
      22 *Cf.* xi. 14.
      23 Or probably, more generally, an apposite utterance of any kind (not necessarily an *answer*). *Cf.* xvi. 1.
      24 No allusion to heaven.
      26 Emended text: " delight " (in frequent antithesis with " abomination ": *cf.* xii. 22), instead of " pure," which gives little sense and no sort of contrast with first line.
      27 Practically = " bribes." The reference is to judges (in first line, unscrupulous). *Cf.* xvii. 23.
      28 So LXX., for the almost impossible " studies *to answer*."
      30 *I.e.*, the eyes of the bringer of good news. *Cf. b.*
      31 Lit. " reproof of life " *i.e.*, which leads to life.
      33*b* = xviii. 12*b*.

XVI. 1 More than " answer." *Cf.* xv. 23.
      2 *Cf.* xxi. 2.
      5 *Cf.* note on xi. 21*a*.
      6 *I.e.*, the disaster which overtakes sin. Or " turn from evil."
      10 *Vv.* 10—15 gather round the *king*. *Cf.* xxv. 2—7.
      11 Hebrew " *just* scales." Perhaps omit " just," as in second line *all* weights (*i.e.*, the whole system) are His. Or we may read *judgment* : " touching balance and scales the Lord *decideth*."
          Perhaps originally *the king's*, *i.e.*, established by the king. *Cf.* second line. The whole context deals with kings (*vv.* 10—15).

Proverbs

In which they were customarily carried by the merchant.

17 Or, "the path of the upright lies in the shunning of evil, and he who would guard his life must give heed to his ways."

18 *Cf.* xi. 2 ; xviii. 12.

20 Of the wise, or of God (in the Torah, *i.e.*, Scripture ?).

25 = xiv. 12.

XVII. 3 = xxvii. 21*a*.

5 *Cf.* xiv. 31.

7 By the change of a letter, for " excellent."

8 Lit. " a stone *of favour*," *i.e.*, which procures favour.

10 Two roots are possible—either "descends into" or "terrifies": in either case = "makes more impression."

11 A messenger from "the Lord" (so LXX.), *i.e.*, in the shape of some misfortune. But if the rebellion of *a* be political, the line (by the omission of one letter) may be rendered, "*the king* sends a cruel messenger against him."

14 LXX. reads "words" for "water" (by change of one letter). The Hebrew, "the beginning of strife is the letting out (?) of water," is taken to mean that strife, like water, is easy to start, but difficult to check. Meaning of last word uncertain.

18 *I.e.*, pledges himself.
Cf. vi. 1—5 ; xi. 15.

19 By change of a letter from "transgression," which, if retained, would apparently = "punishment." Lit. "raises his *gate* (LXX. *house*) high." Frankenberg changes "gate" to "mouth" (=" *speaks loftily* "). So Toy.

23 Hebrew adds "from the bosom " (*i.e.*, of the dress of the man who offers it).

26 The couplet is somewhat obscure, especially the second line (and the *even* of the first line is more than doubtful). The second line has been emended to mean " (It is not right) to oppress him in court unjustly."

XVIII. 1 The meaning of the verse is very obscure. The first line reads in LXX., " a man who wishes to separate from friends seeks excuses."

Notes

So LXX., by change of a letter, for " desire."
2 Lit. " in revealing his heart " (LXX. " folly ").
4 So LXX. and some Hebrew MSS. for " wisdom."
8 = xxvi. 22.
9 *Cf.* xxviii. 24*b*.
10 Lit. "the *name* (=personality) of the Lord."
11*a* = x. 15*a*.
By a simple change, which gives an admirable parallelism : instead of " in his estimation." So Frankenberg.
12*a Cf.* xvi. 18*a*.
b = xv. 33*b*.
15 Not a repetition of, but a parallel to, *knowledge* is naturally to be expected.
19 This translation is founded on Toy's reconstruction of the verse which he regards as ultimately a possible variant of *v.* 11 (*cf.* x. 15). The text and translation of the verse, as it stands, are absolutely hopeless. The meaning commonly put upon the Hebrew is unwarranted and all but impossible : " a brother sinned against is (harder to be won) than a strong city ; and (such or their) contentions are like the bars of a palace." LXX. reads, " a brother helped by a brother is like a strong and lofty city, and is as strong as a well-founded palace."
21 LXX. " control," by a slight change : in that case, *shall* eat.
24 R.V., " he that maketh many friends doeth it to his own destruction " is possible, but does not give so good an antithesis.

XIX. 1 Almost = xxviii. 6.
" In his *words* " (lit. *lips*) : "in his *ways*" (*cf.* xxviii. 6) would make a better parallel to " he who *walks* " in first line.
So xxviii. 6 (instead of " a fool "). This makes a better and almost necessary antithesis to " poor " in first line.
2 Lit. " not good." The exact meaning of this line is greatly disputed.
4 Or " the poor man is separated from his friend."
5 Almost = *v.* 9. *Cf.* xxi. 28.

Proverbs

7 The third line is unintelligible. LXX. has it in another form, and other three lines as well.
8 Because wisdom leads to life. Or we may render " he loveth *himself*," *i.e.*, he is his own true friend.
12 *Cf.* xx. 2*a*.
13 *Cf.* xxvii. 15.
16 For "his ways," by a simple change : makes better parallelism. *Cf.* xiii. 13.
18 Lit. "on bringing him to death," which is the result of lack of discipline. The words can hardly be taken as a warning against *killing* a son. *Cf.* xxiii. 13.
19 Frankenberg's emended text. Text and meaning—especially of second line—extremely uncertain. For *b*, *cf.* xxi. 11.
20 Or " in thy *ways* "—by slight transposition of letters (so Syriac).
22 So LXX. (fruit). Exact meaning of line uncertain.
24 Almost = xxvi. 15.
25 *Cf.* xxi. 11.
27 By a simple change, for "to hear" (so Frankenberg). But as the address "my son," common in chs. i.—ix., nowhere else occurs in this section of the Book (and is not supported here by LXX., which reads " *a* son who ceases, etc."), Toy has suggested, " *He who* ceases to listen to instruction will wander, etc."
28 By the change of a letter, for "swallows."
29 So LXX., by the change of a letter, for "judgments."

XX. 1 Or " is not wise."
2 *Cf.* xix. 12*a*.
8 *Cf. v.* 26.
10 *Cf. v.* 23 ; xi. 1.
11 By change and transposition of a letter, from "right."
16 Lit. "take his garment, *for* he has gone bail, etc.; to illustrate graphically the straits to which a poor man may be reduced (*cf.* Deut. xxiv. 13*f.*) who commits such folly. *Cf.* vi. 1—5. The verse is repeated in xxvii. 13.
Or " him."
19*a* = xi. 13*a* (slight grammatical difference in Hebrew).
23 *Cf. v.* 10 ; xi. 1.

Notes

25 So LXX.: meaning uncertain.
26 *Cf. v.* 8.
Of the threshing cart. *Cf.* first line.
28 So LXX., for " kindness."
30 So LXX. (" befell ") ; but the exact meaning of the verse is uncertain.

XXI. 2 *Cf.* xvi. 2.
3 *Cf. v.* 27; xv. 8; xvi. 6; Amos v. 24*f*; Hos. vi. 6; Isa. i. 11—17; Micah vi. 6—8; Isa. lviii. 5—8; Pss. xl. 6*ff*; l. 9*ff*.; li. 16*f*.
4 Lit. " fallow-ground," LXX. " lamp." The meaning of the phrase is obscure.
6 The translation of this verse rests on LXX. (which, however, reads " *on* deadly snares ").
8 Meaning and text very uncertain.
9 = xxv. 24. *Cf. v.* 19.
I.e., in a simple tiny room which was sometimes built there. *Cf.* 1 Kings xvii. 19 ; 2 Kings iv. 10.
11 *Cf.* xix. 25.
12 Meaning of verse very uncertain. Lit. " the righteous considers the house of the wicked, he overturns the wicked to ruin." The second sentence suggests that the " righteous " in first line is God ; but this use of the word would be unexampled, and is not really justified by Job xxxiv. 17. Perhaps " Jehovah " ought to be substituted. So Toy.
14 Meaning uncertain.
16 Lit. " the Shades." *Cf.* ii. 18 ; ix. 18.
18 *Cf.* xi. 8.
19 *Cf. v.* 9.
20 " and oil "—perhaps gloss (or intrusion from *v.* 17). LXX. " will rest (dwell)."
21 With LXX. omit " justice."
26 Meaning uncertain. LXX. " the ungodly cherishes (lit. desires) evil desires all the day."
28 *Cf.* xix. 5, 9.
Something like this appears to be the meaning ; but the text, as it stands, yields no satisfactory sense.
29 Or " consider " : or, by dropping a tittle, " *establish* their way."
30 *I.e.*, " compare with " or " avail against." *Cf. v.* 31.

Proverbs

XXII. 2 *Cf.* xxix. 13.
    3 = xxvii. 12.
    5 For " thorns," by change of one letter.
    6 In the way he *is to go* (hardly " in the way he *should* go.") Possibly " in accordance with his *bent*."
    8 So in part LXX.
  11 So LXX.
Or, by transposing " the king " to first line, and with a suggestion from LXX., " The king loveth the pure in heart, And grace of lips is his delight."
  12 Exact meaning of line doubtful.
  13 *Cf.* xxvi. 13.
  14 *Cf.* xxiii. 27*a*.
  16 The translation and meaning of this verse are greatly disputed.
  17 The proverbs in this collection are usually in the form of quatrains (two verses of two lines each) though sometimes they are longer.
The text of *vv.* 17—21 is full of uncertainty, and LXX. often deviates widely. The translation given rests partly on emendation, and partly on suggestions from LXX.
The first person in *vv.* 19*f.* suggests that " the words *of the wise* " should be read " *my* words " (" the wise " having perhaps come into the text from the margin. *Cf.* xxiv. 23).
  21 For " send " : rests on LXX.
  26 *Cf.* vi. 1—5.
  27 So LXX., which has no " why ? "
XXIII. 1 Or " what."
    4 *V.* 3 is probably not original. $3a = 6b$, and $3b$ comes naturally after $8a$. (So Toy.)
    5 *I.e.*, the riches. The phrase is almost identical in the Hebrew with Job vii. 8*b*. The first word " shall it fly ? " seems to be an inadvertent intrusion from the last line of the verse.
    7 The meaning of this line, which appears in the Hebrew too long for a single line and too short for a couplet, is very uncertain.
  10 Lit. " ancient," and the line = xxii. 28*a*. But a very slight change gives " widow's," and the parallelism " fatherless " almost demands this.

Notes

13 "If (or though) thou beat him with the rod, he will not *die.*" This has not the humorous meaning, "there is no fear of your *killing* him." It means, as *v.* 14 shows, his fate will not be that death which is inevitable to the unchastised. *Cf.* xix. 18.

19 Emended text.

22 *V.* 23 interrupts the connection and is not in LXX. It runs: "Buy the truth, and sell it not; Wisdom instruction and insight."

27 *Cf.* xxii. 14*a*.
Lit. " alien ": see note on ii. 16.

34 So in part LXX. The text of this verse (esp. of second line) is highly uncertain. LXX. "like a pilot in a heavy surge."

35 This is what the drunkard says, like the sluggard in vi. 10.

XXIV. 5 So LXX.

10 The translation in A.V. and R.V. is pure tautology.

12 So Latin version.

14 The rest of the verse (except "If thou hast found it ") is identical with xxiii. 18, and appears here to be an intrusion from that verse.

15 Omit " O wicked man " as a metrically superfluous gloss: besides, the appeal of this section is to the *pupil*. *Cf.* xxii. 17—21.

21 By two simple changes, supported by LXX.

23 *Cf.* xxviii. 21*a*.

26 *I.e.*, a straightforward answer is a kind and friendly act.

27 Some here insert "take thee a wife." The meaning is "Be prepared to earn your bread before founding a family."

33*f* = vi. 10*f*.

XXV. 2 *Vv.* 2—7*b* deal with kings. *Cf.* xvi. 10—15.

4 So LXX.

11 Or, by a transposition of consonants, "graved work."

15 For "ruler," by change of a letter.
I.e., the hardest opposition can be overcome.

20 The letters of the first clause (which we have left untranslated) practically repeat those of the last clause of *v.* 19.
So LXX. for "soda."

Proverbs

24 = xxi. 9.
27 By an emendation of Frankenberg's, resting on LXX.
XXVI. 3 Cf. 13b.
6 Lit. " violence, wrong." LXX. " reproach."
7 Meaning uncertain.
8 Meaning of line uncertain.
9 Precise meaning of line uncertain.
10 So substantially LXX. The Hebrew text of the verse, as it stands, is untranslatable.
12b = xxix. 20b.
13 Cf. xxii. 13.
15 Cf. xix. 24.
22 = xviii. 8.
23 LXX. " smooth," by the change of one letter.
28 Toy's emendation. Text uncertain and improbable.
XXVII. 6 *I.e.*, and insincere. *Cf.* Judas in Matt. xxvi. 49. Or, by change of text, " deceitful " (so A.V.), which makes better antithesis.
9 This translation rests on LXX.
10 But *cf* xvii. 17.
12 = xxii. 3.
13 = xx. 16. " Strange woman " (*fem.*) of the text should be altered to *masc.* (pl. or sing.), " stranger " (= other).
15 Cf. xix. 13.
16 Suggesting the woman's elusiveness. This translation of the verse, which is precarious and uncertain in every particular, assumes the connection of this verse with the preceding ; but this is very doubtful. LXX. reads altogether differently :
"The north is a wind that is harsh,
  But by name it is called auspicious."
19 The word rendered in A.V. and R.V. " as in water," should be altered, by dropping a letter, to the simple " as."
It is not clear from the Hebrew whether the point lies in the likeness or the unlikeness of men to one another.
20 Cf. xv. 11, and note on Job xxvi. 6.
21a = xvii. 3a.

Notes

24 For "crown," by simple change. *Cf.* Jer. xx. 5.
27 "(And) for the food of thy household" spoils the metre and is not in LXX.

XXVIII. 2 So LXX., by slight changes. The Hebrew is obviously wrong in many particulars.
3 So LXX. for "poor" (by addition of a letter).
4 Or "the law" (of Jehovah) in Scripture. *Cf. vv.* 7, 9.
6 Almost = xix. 1.
7 Or "the law." *Cf. vv.* 4, 9.
8 Interest—on loans of money; increase—on loans of food. *Cf.* Lev. xxv. 37.
12 Or, by emendation, "tremble." Meaning uncertain. *Cf. v.* 28a, where the word, however, is different.
14 *I.e.*, feareth God.
17 Toy's suggested emendations. The text as it stands (see A.V. and R.V.) has one unexampled usage, conveys little meaning (what is *the pit* in this connection?), and in two important particulars is not supported by LXX. "Apprehend" may also be rendered "support."
18 Uncertain: perhaps (by emendation) "into the pit."
19 *Cf.* xii. 11.
21 *I.e.*, in administering justice. *Cf.* xxiv. 23.
22 Lit. "a man of evil eye."
24 *Cf.* xviii. 9b.
25 See note on xiii. 4.
28 *Cf. v.* 12b.

XXIX. 9 *I.e.*, the fool. Or (if *he* be the wise man), "whether he speak in anger or mockery, there is no quiet," *i.e.*, no end to the dispute; or, "it does not terrify" (so LXX.), *i.e.*, it makes no impression.
10 For "the upright"—by addition of one letter and transposition.
11 Emended text, resting partly on LXX.
13 *Cf.* xxii. 2.
19 Any more than a son; both need the rod. *Cf. v.* 15; xix. 18; xxiii. 13.
20b = xxvi. 12b.
21 So LXX., which gives much better sense than the Hebrew (whose last word is altogether obscure).
24 *I.e.*, makes no declaration, discloses nothing.

Proverbs

XXX. 1 *I.e.*, of Massa (in north Arabia ?). Or the word may mean " the prophetic oracle." The meaning is very uncertain, and the word is possibly not original.
With his meditations on the world-problem.
3 Is this an agnostic allusion to ix. 10*b* ?
4 Ironical (*cf.* Job xxxviii. 5). But this line is not in LXX.
5 *Vv.* 5*f* may be a (later ?) pious answer to the seemingly idle speculations of *vv.* 2—4.
Or " are pure."
15 The first sentence, which is very obscure, appears to have been the beginning of an unfinished proverb, which drew an illustration from the leech. " The leech (or vampire ?) hath two daughters—give, give."
For the arithmetical enumerations in *vv.* 15—31, *cf.* note on vi. 16.
16 The form of the verse (which has only *three* lines, not four) renders it probable that here some words have fallen out, such as, " never sated with dead." *Cf.* xxvii. 20.
17 So LXX.
19 The following verse (20) has been appended under the influence of a misinterpretation of the last clause of *v.* 19, where the reference is only to the *mystery* or miracle of procreation. It runs as follows :—
Even so is the way of the adulteress :
She eateth and wipeth her mouth,
Saying, " What I have done is no sin."
22 " Of bread " : but the application is more general—to riches.
23 Lit. " hated," *i.e.*, unattractive (rather than divorced).
24 So LXX., reading same consonants, but different vowels.
28 Lit. " grasp."
31 Emended text.
So LXX. But meaning extremely uncertain.
The line is desperate and the meaning wholly obscure. The idea may be something like that here suggested (*cf.* Job. xxix. 25), which rests on conjecture and emended text. Nothing, however, is plain but the

Notes

word for "king," and even that may not be original. There may have stood in this line the name and description of some majestic *animal*.

32 So, roughly, Frankenberg. But the verse is exceedingly obscure and LXX. is quite different.

33 There are word-plays here which it is impossible to reproduce. " Churning " and " wringing " represent *one* word in Hebrew—" pressing " ; and the word rendered " wrath " is the dual of the word for " nose."

XXXI. 1 Very uncertain. *Cf.* note on xxx. 1.
2 This translation rests in part on LXX.
3 By a simple change, for " ways."
4 By addition of one letter to word rendered in R.V by *where ?*
8 Slight emendation. The Hebrew reads " dumb," which, though making good sense, leaves a difficulty with the following word ("*to* the cause of, etc.") and clause, which is overcome by the emendation.

A phrase of very uncertain meaning. By the dropping of a letter it would mean " sons of sickness, suffering."

10 This is an alphabetic poem (*vv.* 10—31)—the verses beginning (like Ps. xxv. ; Lam. i. ii., iv.) with successive letters of the Hebrew alphabet.
18 Symbol of prosperity (*cf.* xiii. 9 ; xxiv. 20 ; Job xviii. 6) rather than of industry.
21 Which was warm.
30 Lit. " of understanding " (so LXX.). This is more in accordance than the Hebrew " that feareth the Lord " with the previous sketch, which has no religious traits, though doubtless in *Proverbs* practical wisdom is indissolubly associated with " the fear of the Lord," *i.e.*, religion. *Cf.* i. 7 ; ix. 10.

ECCLESIASTES

I. 1 Meaning uncertain. In any case, hardly " preacher " ; possibly an official speaker (president ?) in an assembly—the assembly conceived perhaps as those who have ears to hear the words of wisdom.

Clearly Solomon is intended. Famous alike for his wisdom and his wealth (with the opportunities for

Ecclesiastes

pleasure which his wealth afforded), he is fittingly chosen by the very late writer of this book (about 200 B.C.) as the mouthpiece of his reflections on life.

2 The untranslatable word here rendered "vanity" rings like a knell throughout the whole book from beginning (i. 2) to end (xii. 8). It means primarily *vapour, breath* and graphically characterises the *unsubstantial* quality of things, and so suggests ideas like *nothingness, hollowness, illusion, futility,* even *anomaly* (*cf.* viii. 14). The melancholy repetition of the Hebrew word is very impressive; but, considering the vagueness and breadth of its meaning, I have deliberately refrained from rendering it uniformly.

There are differences of opinion as to the extent of the metrical element in Ecclesiastes, but there is a general agreement that parts of it are metrical.

5 With *vv.* 5—8 contrast the jubilant tone of the Nature Psalms xix, civ. (viii.).

II. 3 And therefore able to estimate his experiences critically and impartially. *Cf. v.* 9.

12 An exceedingly obscure sentence. It may mean: an incompetent successor will follow the habit of Oriental kings and rule without intelligence. (So Siegfried, whose transposition of the two halves of *v.* 12 I have adopted.) Some detect here, perhaps needlessly, a reference to the foolish Rehoboam (1 Kings xii.). Others translate: What *can* the king's successor do? etc., and explain: No successor can have a wider opportunity for experiments than King Solomon himself.

25 So LXX., by a simple and probable change, instead of "who can eat or have enjoyment more than I?"

26 It is very generally agreed that, in later times, the book was touched in places, as here, by pious scribes who, offended and alarmed by the original writer's pessimism and by his dangerous challenge of the moral order, inserted passages which affirmed that order and the certainty of retributive justice in this, or the future, world. These passages are printed in smaller type and at a distance from the margin, so that the original book, together with their effect upon it, becomes clear.

Notes

III. 5   Perhaps to mar the soil, as in time of war. *Cf.* 2 Kings iii. 19, 25.

Lit. " to gather " : perhaps to gather and clear them away from the soil, as in Isa. v. 2.

11   This seems one of the pious insertions (*cf.* ii. 26)—a protest against the thought of *vv.* 1—8. There the order of the world is vexatious and profitless (*cf. v.* 9) because it is *fixed*, and one thing is not merely replaced by, but negated by, another: here the order is regarded as a *fair*, fine, beautiful order.

Meaning extremely uncertain. It may be "the future" or, by a very simple change, "ignorance (so that man cannot discern), etc."; or possibly, by a transposition of consonants, "toil." *Cf.* Gen. iii.

12   Apparently "to fare well" rather than "to do good."

14   See note on ii. 26.

15   Lit. " been driven."

17   Or, " for there is a time (*i.e.*, of judgment) *there*," whether (*a*) with God, or (*b*) in the future world, or (*c*) at some future time in this world.

See note on ii. 26. The verse is a manifest protest against the alarmingly sceptical context.

21   So LXX., which is certainly correct. The translation " Who knoweth the spirit of man *which* goeth upward, and the spirit of the beast *which* goeth downward " is a dogmatic correction, skilfully secured by a very slight change of vowels.

IV. 4   Lit. " is, *i.e.*, involves, jealousy "—whether as cause or consequence or both ?

5   Apparently = " brings himself to ruin." This verse is generally believed to be a later protest against the following verse, which seemed to encourage indolence :—it is *the fool* who so behaves. With the following translation, which is just possible, though hardly probable, the verse might be retained as integral to the context and to the original book:

" The fool foldeth his hands,
    Yet he eateth meat of his own "—

i.e., he has more enjoyment than the laborious toiler.

V. 1   Or, " to draw near *to obey*." *Cf.* 1 Sam. xv. 22.

Ecclesiastes

3 *I.e.*, the idle clatter of *vows*. *Cf.* Matt. vi. 6*f*.
6 The phrase "to cause thy flesh *to sin*" carries with it the idea of *punishment* as well—*physical* punishment. *Cf. flesh.*
Lit. "the messenger" (*i.e.*, of God)—apparently the priest. *Cf.* Mal. ii. 7.
7 By transposing two words: but the meaning is uncertain.
8 Or "another," *i.e.*, the king:—hardly (though not impossibly) God.
9 Meaning very uncertain.
14 Lit. "there is nothing in his (*i.e.*, the father's?) hand." Or, less probably: "and, if he beget a son, there is nothing in his (*i.e.*, *the son's*) hand "— the son is heir to nothing.
17 So LXX. for "he eateth."
20 Meaning very uncertain. The verb may mean either "answer" or "occupy," and the meaning may be "God answereth by giving him gladness of heart" or (with a slight change) "God occupieth his heart with joy" (which helps him to forget the misery of existence).

VI. 6 Sheol. *I.e.*, since beyond death there is nothing, if there is no happiness here, he can have none at all.
10 Lit. "is (already) *known*," fore-known, practically = fore-ordained.
11 *I.e.*, discussions (which must necessarily be futile, *cf.* v. 10) about the divine government of the world. Or, "there are many things" (*e.g.*, knowledge, wealth, pleasure, etc.) "which (but go to) increase (the) futility (of life)."

VII. 1 In Hebrew there is a play on the words *name* and *ointment*: *name* and *nard* have been suggested.
2 *I.e.*, death.
3 *I.e.*, pessimism is the true wisdom. This translation, which is in harmony with the pervasive mood of the book, is more probable than "by the sadness of the countenance the heart is made *glad*." Or possibly: "sadness of countenance is good for the heart," which matures in sorrow.
6 Play upon words. *Cf. v.* 1.

Notes

7 The verse begins with *for*, but there is no apparent connection : perhaps something has been lost.
Lit. *heart*, *i.e.*, the intellectual and moral nature.

11 This meaning seems to be confirmed by the following verse (12) ; but it may also be rendered, " Wisdom with (*i.e.*, accompanied by) an inheritance is good, etc."—*i.e.*, the combination of wealth with the wisdom which enables its possessor to enjoy it.

14 Or, " for the reason that there is no experience for man beyond death."

15 Same word as is used throughout the book for " futility, illusion, vanity "—" my transient, evanescent days," " my days of illusion."

18 The Pharisaic principle of *v.* 16.
The Sadducean principle of *v.* 17.
Meaning slightly uncertain : apparently the joyless life of a punctilious and mechanical piety on the one hand, and the ruin to which laxity leads on the other. True religion is compatible with temperate enjoyment : it avoids asceticism and sensuality alike.

19 Or (by a change of vowels) " than *the wealth* of the men in authority, etc."

20 Connection often obscure (*cf. v.* 7), perhaps owing to original order having been disturbed by interpolations.

VIII. 3 Or, joining this sentence to the last, " be in no haste to leave his presence."
E.g., conspiracy, or—more simply—disobedience to the royal order.

5 Of God ? or the king ?
Or " can have no kinship with evil." *Cf.* Ps. ci. 4*b*. *Cf.* ch. iii.

6 Lit. " the calamity (or wickedness or misery) of *man* is great upon him "—a general statement apparently intended to have a particular application to the tyrant ; but the meaning is very obscure, perhaps intentionally so. Despotism (*cf. v.* 9) made free speech dangerous (*cf.* x. 20).

10 Apparently the temple.
Text uncertain. With another reading we may translate : " I saw wicked men buried (with honour) and entering (into rest ?), while others who had acted

Ecclesiastes

honestly had to leave the holy place (*i.e.*, Jerusalem : for exile ?), and they passed into oblivion in the city." The first clause Cheyne, following Bickell, translates : "I have seen ungodly men honoured, and that too in the holy place (*i.e.*, the temple) ; but those who had acted rightly had to depart, etc." (*Job and Solomon*, p. 220.)

11—13 These verses, insisting upon the doctrine of retribution, are a pious protest against the sceptical context. *Cf.* note on ii. 26.

The shadow (*cf.* vi. 12) is a symbol of transitoriness ; but it may mean, " shall not prolong his days like the (evening) shadow."

14 The word which rings throughout the book—vanity, futility. *Cf.* note on i. 2.

16 Is he thinking of himself ? or, in general, of toiling humanity ? or of the sleepless activity of *God ?* — "*He* sees no sleep day or night."

IX. 1 So LXX.

It is not clear whether the reference is to *men's* own love or hatred (the " doings " just mentioned) or to *God's*.

So LXX.

2 So LXX.

In the other groups the superior character comes first ; but the meaning may be, " those who take oaths (lightly or rashly) and those who reverence them."

3 Transpose " is joined " from *v.* 4 to *v.* 3 ; and for "*whosoever*" (is joined) at the beginning of *v.* 4 read, by a very slight change, " who will be left, survive ? " (So Podechard.)

4 Despised in the Orient.

5 Strange superiority. Apparently the meaning is :— and, with this certainty in view, can plan to enjoy life while it lasts.

7 Or, " for God has approved (*i.e.*, shown His approval) of thy works," *i.e.*, of thy toil, *viz.*, by giving thee the opportunity of enjoyment.

8 Worn on festal occasions.

9 *I.e.*, God.

Notes

16 This verse seems to contradict *v.* 15. Dr. A. H. McNeile secures harmony by rendering *v.* 15—" and he *would have delivered* the city by his wisdom." But *v.* 16 may be regarded as a general statement, describing the world's attitude to the poor wise man when the crisis is over, or when there is no crisis.

18 So Syriac: also makes better parallelism (*cf.* x. 1). Hebrew text reads "one (man) who sins," *i.e.*, blunders.

X. 2 Practically = leads him *right* (*i.e.*, in the right direction), as *left*, in the next clause = wrong.

3 So, after LXX. The Hebrew reads, "he saith to (or *of*) every one that he is a fool."

4 Lit. " sins."

5 Earth's Ruler seems to this pessimistic writer as capricious as an Oriental despot.

15 Meaning uncertain. Perhaps it is the fool himself who does not know his way to the town:—reading instead of *who* " for he (*i.e.*, the fool) does not know, etc."

20 Or, " even among thine *acquaintance*." Or possibly, by a simple change, " even on thy *bed*," which also makes a better parallelism. The verse refers to the elaborate system of espionage.

XI. 2 An exhortation to generosity. Or it may be, " divide thy possessions into seven, yea eight portions," like our " don't put all your eggs into one basket."

3 Or possibly a stick, used in divination (*cf.* Hos. iv. 12). If it " is tossed up in the air, that a man may guide his action by the direction in which it comes to rest, he has no control over the result " (A. H. McNeile).

5 Lit. " bones " = frame-work.

9 These two lines are probably a pious interpolation. *Cf.* note on ii. 26.

10 Lit. " what is evil," *i.e.*, ascetic practices. Or the " dark hair," *i.e.*, of youth.

XII. 1 The first two lines are probably another pious interpolation. *Cf.* note on xi. 9.
" Young manhood " rather than " youth."

2 Lit. " while the sun is not (yet) dark."

3 Probably the arms and hands. The legs.

Lamentations

The maidens who grind, *i.e.*, the teeth.
The ladies who look, etc., *i.e.*, the eyes.
4 Lips ? (Jaws ? Ears ?)
The (grinding) mill, *i.e.*, the mouth.
Or faintly heard. Emended text.
Lit. " sunk."
5 A reference perhaps to the old man's white hair.
Meaning very uncertain.
I.e., powerless to excite desire. Or the meaning may
be " bursts." *Cf.* LXX.
11 Meaning very uncertain. Lit. " the words of wise
men are like goads, or like nails planted by " (with
the addition of a single letter) " the lords of collection," *i.e.*, the collectors (of the words ?).
God (or Solomon ?).

LAMENTATIONS

I. There is no warrant in the Hebrew text for assigning the book to Jeremiah, nor is it very probable that he was the author. In the Hebrew Bible, the book is not placed after Jeremiah nor indeed among the prophets at all, but in the third and last division of the Old Testament books (the so-called *Writings*), usually—in the printed editions—between Ruth and Ecclesiastes. The Greek version, however, introduces the book thus: " And it came to pass, after Israel had been led captive and Jerusalem made desolate, that Jeremiah sat down weeping, and lifted up this lament over Jerusalem and said." See my *Introduction to the Old Testament* (pp. 295*ff.*). The first four chapters are alphabetic (*cf.* Ps. xxv.), and there is consequently, as a rule, little continuity of thought. They are elegies, written in the elegiac metre, in which the second line is shorter than the first—usually three beats followed by two.

1 In chs. I. and II. the strophes (which begin with successive letters of the Hebrew alphabet) consist o three lines (each with a longer and a shorter half).
4 So LXX. Hebrew " are in grief " (afflicted).

Notes

7 The metre makes it highly probable that the second clause is an interpolation: "all her pleasant things that were from the days of old."
9 The translation follows Budde's slight, but highly probable, readjustment of the lines in vv. 8 and 9.
10 Bickell's addition—for metrical reasons.
12 The beginning of the verse is very uncertain.
15 To the enemy the annihilation of Israel is a festival to which they have been summoned, as it were, by Jehovah Himself.
19 An easy and probable addition, demanded by the metre.
So LXX. The present ending is apparently an intrusion from v. 11b.
20 Lit. death, i.e., deadly plague.
21 I.e., through the prophets.
22 The translation rests on a probable readjustment of the lines in vv. 21 and 22.

II. 1 Chs. ii. and iv. are probably the earliest poems of the book. They are so graphic as to look almost like a transcript by an eye-witness.
Either the ark (cf. 1 Chron. xxviii. 2) or, more generally, the temple.
2 So LXX.: for "the kingdom."
4 Omit "His right hand."
The second half of the line appears to have been lost.
6 I.e., temple and people. Cf. Isa. i. 8; Ps. lxxx. 8ff. So LXX. Dyserinck proposes, by addition of one letter, "His booth He has ravaged like *a thief*." Sir George Adam Smith, "He hath torn from his Garden his Booth" (*Jerusalem*, vol. ii. p. 275).
7 Or possibly some word which indicated the buildings of the temple. Dyserinck: "the walls of His dwelling-place." Budde: "His ark of the covenant."
9 I.e., instruction from *the priests*. Cf. *prophets* in next line: see Jer. xviii. 18; Ezek. vii. 26.
11 Lit. "liver."
15 The rest of the line, "the joy of the whole earth," appears to be a (marginal) intrusion from Ps. xlviii. 2.
18 Emended text.

276

Lamentations

19 The line "that swoon for hunger at the head of all the streets" is metrically superfluous and probably a later addition, suggested by vv. 11 and 12.

22 Or "terrors."

III. Throughout this poem, *each* line within the strophe (which consists of *three* verses) begins with the same of the alphabet.

1 To be taken collectively of the people (*cf.* vv. 40—47), as often in the Psalms (*cf.* Ps. cxxix. 1).

16 *I.e.*, (i.) He gave me stones instead of bread, or gritty bread; or (ii.) thrown to the ground, I gnawed the stones in my pain; or (iii.) the reference may be to some punishment.

19 So Budde, by a slight and (in the context) probable change in the punctuation.

28 Or "for."

31 So A. R. Gordon (*Poets of the Old Testament*, p. 94). Budde supplies less well "man" or "the children of men" (*cf.* v. 33). Some such addition seems metrically necessary.

34 This long and somewhat infelicitous sentence (vv. 34—36) is due to the necessities of the alphabetic acrostic.

36 Or, by the change of a letter, "the Lord disapproves."

41 Lit. "on," *i.e.*, openly. Or, possibly, "*not* our hands." *Cf.* Joel ii. 13.

42 This is the beginning of the prayer (vv. 42—47).

51 Meaning of the verse a little uncertain.

63 *I.e.*, in the whole course of their life. *Cf.* Ps. cxxxix. 2. Deut. vi. 7.

65 Or "obstinacy." Meaning uncertain.

IV. In this poem, the strophes (which begin with successive letters of the Hebrew alphabet) consist of *two* lines (unlike chs. i.—iii.). See note on i. 1.

1 The verse may be taken literally of the temple (v. 2 referring to the people of Jerusalem) or, more probably, metaphorically (v. 2 being regarded as the explanation).

2 *I.e.*, worth their weight in gold.

6 This is Sir George Adam Smith's translation of the last two lines (*Jerusalem*, ii. 280). Meaning uncertain.

Notes

7   Text and meaning of last two lines very uncertain.
9   Text and meaning very uncertain.
13 *Cf.* Jer. xxvi. 8, where prophets and priests clamour for Jeremiah's blood.
14 Meaning uncertain. It may be, " Men shrink from them as they stagger by, lest they should contract ceremonial defilement from their garments " (A. S. Peake).
15 Cain's sin and Cain's punishment (Gen. iv. 12, 14).
    Omit " men said among the nations " ; which is irrelevant and metrically superfluous.
16 So LXX., for " elders."
17 *I.e.*, Egypt. *Cf.* Jer. xxxvii. 5*ff.*
20 Zedekiah. *Cf.* 2 Kings xxv. 4*f.*
    Lit. " pits " (with stakes fixed in them).
    I.e., under his protection. *Cf.* Ps. cxxi. 5.
    Lit. " among the nations." This may mean, " even if we should be driven from our land, and compelled to live in the country east of the Jordan " (or even in Babylon, as exiles ?). But it may also mean, " have our independent place as a nation *among the nations* of the world."
21 " Uz," which is not in LXX., is apparently a gloss.
    For a similar threat on Edom (in connection with Jerusalem's experience at the hands of Babylon), *cf.* Ps. cxxxvii. 7.

V. This poem is not, like chs. i.—iv., alphabetic ; but it can be no accident that the number of verses in it coincides with the number of letters in the Hebrew alphabet (22).
5   Text uncertain.
6   Perhaps here = Babylon, as later it is used as = Persia (*cf.* Ezra vi. 22, where Darius is referred to as king of *Assyria* : *cf.* ix. 9) and possibly later still as = Syria (*cf.* Isa. xix. 23—25).

THE SONG OF SONGS

I. 1 *I.e.*, " the loveliest, most charming song." *Cf.* holy of holies = most holy ; servant of servants = the lowliest, most abject slave.

The Song of Songs

This is the first of the songs. " The true view of this perplexing book appears to be that it is, as Herder called it, ' a string of pearls '—an anthology of love or wedding songs sung during the festivities of the ' King's week,' as the first week after the wedding is called in Syria." The bride and bridegroom are " king and queen." For the space of a week the peasant bridegroom is Solomon (*cf.* iii. 7, 9) and his peasant bride is the fair maid of Shulem (vi. 1, 13 ; *cf.* 1 Kings i. 3). " There is a charming naïveté, and indeed something much profounder, in this temporary transformation of those humble rustic lives. . . . This origin of the songs explains the looseness of the arrangement, no attempt being made to unify them, though it may be conceded that the noble eulogy of love in viii. 6*f.*, as it is the finest utterance in the book, was probably intended as a sort of climax." See my *Introduction to the Old Testament*, pp. 285—7.

4 The king is her bridegroom.
5 From sun-burn. *Cf. v.* 6.
6 Perhaps her beauty, which she had exposed to the scorching sun; or, more generally, her charms (or chastity ?).
8 *V.* 8 gives the answer to the question in *v.* 7.
9 The bridegroom speaks.
12 The bride speaks. The king is her bridegroom. Meaning uncertain.
15 The bridegroom speaks.
16 The bride speaks.

II. 1 Or " narcissus " ; hardly " rose."
7 *I.e.*, the lovers ; abstract for concrete.
9 The first sentence of *v.* 9 (" my beloved . . . hart ") is an anticipation of, and probably inserted from, *v.* 17.
By change of a letter, for Hebrew " he."
12 Or " singing."
15 *I.e.*, the maiden's charms (*cf.* i. 6). The four lines constitute a sort of roguish appeal, or perhaps a real appeal for chivalrous protection.
17 Meaning very uncertain.

Notes

III. 4 The last clause ("to the chamber of her that conceived me") appears to belong to viii. 2, which see.

5 See ii. 7.

7—10 This is part of the delightful romantic idealisation of the book. The rustic bridegroom is King Solomon. "Everything is transfigured and takes on the colours of royal magnificence: the threshing board becomes a palanquin, and the rustic bodyguard appear as a band of valiant warriors." See my *Introduction to O.T.*, p. 286.

9 "Solomon" is probably an explanatory gloss.

10 By a very probable emendation (*cf.* Ezek. xxvii. 15) for "love." The phrase "from the daughters of Jerusalem" at the end of the verse appears to have been suggested by "the daughters of Zion" in the next verse.

11 Omit "Solomon": *cf. v.* 9.

IV. 2 Or "All of them casting twins,
And no barren among them."
If this, which is the more literal meaning, be correct, we have simply an instance of a comparison being carried into somewhat irrelevant details.

4 Meaning extremely uncertain. One suggestion is, "As a look-out."

5 The omitted words have apparently been intruded from ii. 16.

6 An allusion probably to the charms just described.

9 It is believed that *v.* 8, which has no very obvious connection with the song in praise of the bride's beauty, is a topographical interpolation resting on a misunderstanding of the allusion to Lebanon in *v.* 11 (and to the hill and mountain of *v.* 6). It runs as follows:—

O bride of mine, come from Lebanon;
O sister, come with me from Lebanon.
Look from the top of Amána,
From the top of Shenír and of Hermon,
From the dens of the lions,
The mountains of panthers.

An endearing name for lover, common in Egyptian love-songs.

The Song of Songs

Meaning very uncertain : lit. "one chain from thy neck." Perhaps, as Gordon (*Poets of the Old Testament*, p. 323) suggests, " one *turn* of thy neck."
16 The bride speaks.
V. 1 The bridegroom accepts the bride's invitation.
3 The bride replies.
4 *I.e.*, of the door.
6 For " spoke."
9 The " daughters of Jerusalem " ask the question.
12 Meaning of verse very obscure. It is not even certain whether the last two lines refer to the eyes (" fitly set " of the English versions) or the doves.
14 Siegfried thinks the allusion is to arm-bangles set with precious stones. Others take the reference to be to the fingers that taper off to the shining nails.
VI. 1 The " daughters of Jerusalem " ask the question.
4 Capital of Northern Israel from Jeroboam I. to Omri.
5—7 Roughly = iv. 2*f*.
8 This substitution of " to Solomon " for " there are " is simple and highly probable (Budde). Solomon would here be the historical king, not the bridegroom. For a similar contrast between the two, *cf*. viii. 11.
9 In contrast with the many in Solomon's harem.
11 *V*. 12 (the text and meaning of which, however, are very uncertain) suggests that *v*. 11 (which seems to be closely connected with it) as well as *v*. 12 are spoken by the bride. The difficulty, however, on this view is that elsewhere, *the bride herself* is the garden (*cf*. iv. 12) which the bridegroom visits (*cf*. vi. 2*f*.)
12 This is the skilful rendering of Professor Gordon (*The Poets of the Old Testament*, p. 325), secured by ingenious, but simple, changes and transpositions. Her lover is the " prince " who captures her. The text and meaning must be regarded, however, as highly uncertain—much too slender to support the dramatic view of the book, which regards it as the story of a peasant maid surprised and captured (*cf*. this verse) by King Solomon's retinue and taken to his harem, but steadily resisting his blandishments and finally restored to her shepherd lover.
13 So the peasant bride is addressed, as though fair as Abisha . *Cf*. note on i. 1.

Notes

Lit. (apparently) " the camp-dance," *i.e.*, the sword-dance—danced by the bride, sword in hand, on the evening of her wedding day. But it may mean " the dance of the two bands," a sort of country-dance; or "the dance of Mahanaim." The meaning is far from certain. In any case the dancing of the bride furnishes the opportunity to describe her beauty in detail, as the question of the Jerusalem women (ch. v. 9) furnished the bride with the opportunity of describing her bridegroom (*vv.* 10—16).

VII. 2 Formerly rendered " navel "; probably " shame."
    4 Or it may be a proper name, " the gate (which leadeth) to Beth-rabbim."
    9 Lit. " palate," *.e.*, mouth : allusion is to kisses. So LXX.
    11 Or " in the *hamlets* " (villages).
VIII. 2 So LXX., a probable reading in the light of the last clause of iii. 4 in the existing text.
Vv. 3 and 4, here irrelevant, seem added from ii. 6*f.* (iii. 5).
    5 Companion picture to iii. 6.
The bridegroom is addressing the bride. (So Syriac.)
So Budde, by the change of a single letter. It is hardly probable that the child was *born* there, as the mother had a house of her own (iii. 4 ; viii. 2). The general idea is probably, as B. suggests, " where thou didst dream thy baby dreams."
    6 The bride speaks.
I.e., seal-ring.
Hardly " jealousy " in this context, but " the passion of love."
Lit. " hard ": *i.e.*, inexorable to the pleadings of another.
Lit. " Sheol," which devours inexorably: " its passion devouring as Sheol."
" Flames of Jah," *i.e.*, of Jehovah, *i.e.*, lightning (1 Kings xviii. 38). So Ewald.
    8 *Vv.* 8 and 9 are apparently spoken by the bride's unamiable brothers, who make a fine foil to her affectionate husband. *Cf.* i. 6.
    9 *I.e.*, if she resists advances, they will reward her.

The Song of Songs

I.e., if she should make herself too accessible, they will take steps to prevent it.

10 The bride's reply, which skilfully turns the brothers' simile (*v*. 9).
I.e., her bridegroom.

11 Here the real historical Solomon with whom the bridegroom (*v*. 12) contrasts himself (*cf*. vi. 8*f*.).

12 The bridegroom speaks. The vineyard is his bride.

13 The bridegroom is addressing the bride.
Vv. 13 and 14 are fragmentary and not very intelligible in the context.

14 Lit. " be," as also in ii. 17*b*, which this verse but repeats. There, however, rest was more naturally implied ; here, motion.

BIBLIOGRAPHY

JOB

A FULL list of books, useful for the study of *Job*, will be found on pp. 293—296 of my volume on *The Problem of Pain—A Study in the Book of Job* (James Clarke & Co., London, 1917). This list includes books of general discussion, commentaries, introductions, and translations. The following brief list is selected as most useful to the general reader:

GENERAL DISCUSSIONS

Aked, C. F. *The Divine Drama of Job*, in *The Short Course* series.
Blake, B. *The Book of Job and the Problem of Suffering*.
Bradley, G. G. *Lectures on the Book of Job*.
Froude, J. A. *Essay on the Book of Job;* now in *Everyman's Library* (Froude's Essays in Literature and History).
Rutherford, M. *Notes on the Book of Job*.

COMMENTARIES

Davidson, A. B., in the *Cambridge Bible* series.
Peake, A. S., in the *Century Bible* series.
Strahan, J. *The Book of Job* (published by T. and T. Clark).

PROVERBS

GENERAL DISCUSSIONS

Cheyne, T. K. *Job and Solomon*, pp. 117—178.
Davidson, A. B., in *Encycl. Britannica;* and in *Book by Book*, pp. 172—184.
Dillon, E. J. Discussion of "Agur the Agnostic," in *Sceptics of the Old Testament*, pp. 131—156.

Bibliography

Elmslie, W. A. L. *Studies in Life from Jewish Proverbs.*
Horton, R. F., in *The Expositor's Bible* series.
Hudal, A. *Die religiösen und sittlichen Ideen des Spruchbuches.*
Kent, C. F. *The Wise Men of Ancient Israel and their Proverbs.*
Nowack, W., in Hastings' *Dictionary of the Bible*, vol. iv.
Toy, C. H., in *Encycl. Biblica.*

COMMENTARIES

Berry, G. R., in *American Commentary on the Old Testament.*
Martin, G. C., in the *Century Bible* series.
Perowne, T. T., in the *Cambridge Bible* series.
Plumptre, E. H., in the *Speaker's Commentary.*
Toy, C. H., in the *International Critical Commentary* series.
Also the Commentaries of Delitzsch, Frankenberg, Nowack, Strack, and Wildeboer.

ECCLESIASTES

GENERAL DISCUSSIONS OF A POPULAR, LITERARY, OR HOMILETIC KIND

Bradley, G. G. *Lectures on Ecclesiastes.*
Cox, S., in the *Expositor's Bible* series.
Devine, M. *Ecclesiastes, or The Confessions of an Adventurous Soul.*
Genung, J. F. *Words of Koheleth.*
Scott, D. R. *Pessimism and Love in Ecclesiastes and the Song of Songs*, in the *Humanism of the Bible* series (James Clarke & Co.).

DISCUSSIONS OF ORIGIN, TEXT, RELATION TO OTHER ANCIENT LITERATURE, &C.

Cheyne, T. K. *Job and Solomon*, pp. 199—285.
McNeile, A. H. *An Introduction to Ecclesiastes.*
Podechard, E. *L'Ecclésiaste*, in *Études Bibliques.*

Bibliography

BRIEFER DISCUSSIONS

Davidson, A. B., in *Book by Book*, pp. 185—192 ; and article in *Encycl. Biblica*.
Dillon, E. J., in *Sceptics of the Old Testament*, pp. 85—129.
Peake, A. S., in Hastings' *Dictionary of the Bible*, vol. 1.

COMMENTARIES

Barton, G. A., in the *International Critical Commentary* series.
Martin, G. C., in the *Century Bible* series.
Plumptre, E. H., in the *Cambridge Bible* series.
Also the Commentaries of C. D. Ginsburg, Siegfried, and Wildeboer.

WISDOM LITERATURE

On the *Wisdom Literature* generally :
Davidson, A. B., in *Biblical and Literary Essays*, pp. 23—81.
Davison, W. T. *The Wisdom Literature of the Old Testament*.
Harvey-Jellie, W. *The Wisdom of God and the Word of God*.
Siegfried, C. Art. *Wisdom*, in vol. iv. of Hastings' *Dictionary of the Bible*.
Toy, C. H. Art. *Wisdom Literature* in *Encycl. Biblica*.

LAMENTATIONS

GENERAL DISCUSSIONS

Adeney, W. F. In the *Expositor's Bible* series.
Cheyne, T. K. *Jeremiah : His Life and Times*, in the *Men of the Bible* series (pp. 177—181).
Art. in *Encycl. Biblica* (some passages by W. R. Smith.)
McFadyen, J. E. The Messages of the Psalmists, in the *Messages of the Bible* series (James Clarke & Co.), pp. 293—313.
Selbie, J. A. Art. in Hastings' *Dictionary of the Bible*.
Smith, W. R. Art. in *Encycl. Britannica*.

Bibliography

COMMENTARIES

Cheyne, T. K., in the *Pulpit Commentary* on Jeremiah and Lamentations.

Ewald, H., in his Commentary on the *Psalms* (English translation), vol. ii., pp. 99—124.

Peake, A. S., in the second vol. of his *Jeremiah* in the *Century Bible* series.

Streane, A. W., in *Jeremiah* and *Lamentations* in the *Cambridge Bible* series.

Also the Commentaries of Budde and Löhr.

TRANSLATIONS

Admirable translations of most of the book will be found in Professor A. R. Gordon's *Poets of the Old Testament*, pp. 79—96 ; and of chs. ii. and iv. in Sir George Adam Smith's *Jerusalem*, vol. ii. pp. 274—283.

THE SONG OF SONGS

GENERAL DISCUSSIONS

Adeney, W. F., in the *Expositor's Bible* series.

Cannon, W. W. *The Song of Songs*, edited as a Dramatic Poem.

Cheyne, T. K. Art. *Canticles* in *Encycl. Biblica*.

Davidson, A. B., in *Book by Book*, pp. 193—197.

Davison, W. T. *The Wisdom Literature of the Old Testament.*

Falconer, H. *The Maid of Shulam.*

Gordon, A. R. *The Poets of the Old Testament*, pp. 309—328.

Haupt, P. *The Book of Canticles ;* and *Biblische Liebeslieder.*

Herder, J. G. *Salomon's Lieder der Liebe.*

Lowth, R. *Lectures on the Sacred Poetry of the Hebrews*—Lectures xxx. and xxxi.

Rothstein, J. W. Art. *Song of Songs* in Hastings' *Dictionary of the Bible.*

Schmidt, N. *The Messages of the Poets* (pp. 213—277) in the *Messages of the Bible* series (James Clarke & Co.).

Smith, W. R. Art. *Canticles* in *Encycl. Britannica.*

Bibliography

COMMENTARIES

Harper, A., in the *Cambridge Bible* series.
Martin, G. C., in the *Century Bible* series.
Also the Commentaries of C. D. Ginsburg, Budde, and Siegfried.

TRANSLATIONS

The book is translated, in whole or in part, in the above-mentioned volumes by Cannon, Ginsburg, Gordon, Harper, and Schmidt; also by T. L. Kingsbury in *The Speaker's Commentary*, and D. R. Scott in *Pessimism and Love in Ecclesiastes and The Song of Songs* (James Clarke & Co.), pp. 235—255.

INTRODUCTIONS

Useful discussions of all the five Old Testament books translated in this volume will be found in the following *Introductions to the Old Testament*:
Driver, S. R., in the *International Theological Library*.
Gray, G. B., in the *Studies in Theology* series.
Mc Fadyen, J. E. (Hodder and Stoughton).
Moore, G. F., in the *Home University Library*.

www.ingramcontent.com/pod-product-compliance
Lightning Source LLC
Chambersburg PA
CBHW032107230426
43672CB00009B/1661